FINAL REPORT

by

Ronald L. Waldron

authorHOUSE®

AuthorHouse™
1663 Liberty Drive, Suite 200
Bloomington, IN 47403
www.authorhouse.com
Phone: 1-800-839-8640

First published by AuthorHouse   12/31/2007

ISBN: 978-1-4343-5892-9 (sc)

Printed in the United States of America
Bloomington, Indiana

This book is printed on acid-free paper.

AMERICANS FOR AMERICA WILL STAY VIGILANT PROTECT OUR CONSTITUTION

EVERY ONE NEEDS TO VOTE IN THE PRIMARIES:

Do not "underestimate" the "anger," "frustration," and "determination," of your citizens who demand "justice and fairness."

The assassination of PRESIDENT JOHN F. KENNEDY Nov. 22, 1963 began my interest in our Country and where it was going. The war on Organized crime, and poverty by the president and, Attorney General Robert Kennedy, Has held my interest to this date.

I became a Police Officer, always keeping in mind the above elements, following the changes in the economy, and political controls that have since taken place.

Trace back, remember private owned businesses, Inter-city conditions and what is now.

The main thing to remember is the president's Famous statement. Ask not what your country can do for you, but what you can do for your Country.

Then, Rev. Martin Luther King. I HAD A DREAM!! The following is the outline as I have seen it.

1

Ronald L. Waldron

I support Barrack Obama as president 2008, because of the similarities to President Kennedy, And a refreshing reality to Rev. Kings dream.

You may not agree, right now we have a right to disagree. BUT we may not have, if we do not protect our Constitution.

The rest of my thoughts:

John Edwards--Vice-President.- One America.
Dennis Kucinich--Secretary of State. What a Statesman.
Joe Biden-- Secretary of Defense. An expert on Foreign Policy.

The Dream Team we need. Not more Polarization.

Thank You for Your Courtesy in reading what I, A plain concerned American Citizen has to say.

I retired after having reported Wrongful activities; my confidential information was exposed, for political motivated, reasoning.

Corruption starts at the local level. Money gained from the illegal markets of Drugs, gambling, pornography, contracts, Special interest invested in free enterprise. Thus effecting the economy. Such travels up the line to county, state, federal levels of Government.

We then end up as we have now. No accountability, ethics, or real moral values.

Citizen review boards, panels, Watch groups need to be established all the way up the line.

Written by a non-professional, but with the same concerns as any citizen wondering what has happened gradually over the last 60 years to end up at a junction with FASCISM....

We need change, not more polarization

Who is accountable for Rubber Stamping the President's disastrous policies for America? Not only republicans give him the green light.

"EDITING" HAS IN REALITY, BECOME "CENSORSHIP"

THINK BEFORE YOU AGREE, BELIEVE WHAT YOU KNOW TO BE "TRUTH".

Question what you hear or read, especially when It involves Politics, Religion, or Corporate manipulation of either.

Does government belong to the people, or people an entity of the Government.

The less you are involved in government, or you're Faith Doctrine, the less separation there is. "MORALITY" Ends up, forgotten.

TRY to think clearly, and then look through a "MAGNIFYING Lens". The "COMMON SENCE" we were all created with seems to come into play.

VOTE ACCORDINGLY, and PRAY for JUSTICE.

Combat "CENSORSHIP" read between the lines.

WORLD DOMINATED PRESS AROUND THE WORLD:
The reaction from the Jewish-dominated press in America and around the world is quite predictable. There has been a crescendo of criticism of Putin and universal defense of the "persecuted" Jewish oligarchs. Putin has even been accused of "anti-Semitism" for prosecuting these criminals.

Because Putin believes that the Russian people should own the press rather than citizens of Israel, he is called an enemy of a free press. Yet, how can any press be free when it is controlled by a people who view themselves more Jewish than Russian and have their own clear international agenda? And today, as Bush calls for Russia to have a free press (translated: the Jewish criminal oligarchs such as Jewish mafia leader Berezovsky should control the press) they call on Russia to pass laws and prosecute Russians who dare to simply criticize the Jewish criminal oligarchs and the their allegiances to Israel and Jewish supremacies rather than to Russia and Russians.

Bush has even had the hypocrisy to criticize Putin for consolidating Russian federal power. In America the federal government literally spends one thousand times more money on the federal government than does Russia. As shocking as that might sound for most Americans to read, it is fact. America spends about 4 trillion on government; Russia spends less than 40 billion! And Bush has the chutzpah to talk about consolidation of power in Russia!

The American government has become the epitome of everything we once opposed. Russia is not communist any more, but the American government, under the domination of the Jewish neocons (who are former communists) acts more and more like the communists have acted for decades.

Bush criticizes Putin and Russian freedom while he works to take away American constitutional freedoms with the Patriot Act.
While the political mafia that controls America kept opposition candidates such as Ralph Nader off many state ballots, Russia had over 20 different parties on the ballot in their National elections.
In America where only two parties control almost the entire political landscape and there's hardly a dime's worth of difference, (such as on the Iraq War) Russia is represented by many parties in their Duma with a wide range of political philosophies and opinions.
Russians of every possible political opinion have representation in the Duma (Congress) while tens of millions of Americans have no voice at all in government for their political opinions. It is precisely why the American founding fathers rebelled against Britain: taxation without representation!

And in the midst of this concerted attack on Putin and Russia, where is the opposition to the still existent, extremely dangerous, still communist nation of China? Patrick Buchanan put it very well in a recent article:

Why are McCain and Lieberman bullyragging Russia but not China? After all, Putin was elected, but Hu Jintao was not. Russia has an elected legislature with opposition parties. China has never held a free election. The Russian people have freedom of religion. China persecutes Christians. Russia threatens no U.S. ally. China threatens Taiwan. In a recent issue of Parade, a list was drawn up of the world's 10 worst dictators based on their human rights violations. Hu Jintao was fourth from the top. Putin was not even mentioned.

There is only one reason for the attacks upon Putin and Russia. Putin and the Russian people dare to defend themselves from the powers of Jewish supremacist. The oligarchs and the Zionists want total supremacy over the Russian nation, and that's why they have made Putin a target. Their puppet George Bush, just as in the Iraq war, is happy to serve these masters of the American political landscape. It is not just leaders of AIPAC that are being investigated for spying who should wear the yellow coat of treason, George Bush has surrendered his presidency completely to this foreign power and shames every real American who has pride in our country.

ORGANIZED CRIME
CONTROL MADE LEGAL??

HYPOCRISY: The political, religious, and corporate Leaders using Faith to promote their AGENDA & RETHORIC for their special interest is what's being QUESTIONED. All are heavily invested in Defense Contracts, contractors, & Military equipment. The Israeli and USA connection, (AIPAC) better Known as Organized Crime Syndicate now being exposed such as it is an Evil domain.

The lobby that Israel and its supporters have built in the United States to make all this aid happen, and to ban discussion of it from the national dialogue, goes far beyond AIPAC, with its $15 million budget, its 150 employees, and its five or six registered lobbyists who manage to visit every member of Congress individually once or twice a year.

AIPAC, in turn, can draw upon the resources of the Conference of Presidents of Major American Jewish Organizations, a roof group set up solely to coordinate the efforts of some 52 national Jewish organizations on behalf of Israel.

AIPAC, or the American Israel Public Affairs Committee, describes itself as the most important organization affecting the U.S. relationship with Israel. With a budget of $65 million, and membership now standing at over 100,000, it is no wonder that congressional staffers consider it one of the most powerful and effective lobbies on Capitol Hill.

This conundrum should have diplomats, parliamentarians, and foreign ministries huddled in their back rooms trying to sort out their own positions, rather than attempting to starve the Palestinians into Hamas's capitulation. For it is not only the funding freeze, that has become rampant nonsense. The entire Road Map logic has become nonsense, too.

Zionists have betrayed all of this, and that is a tragedy not just for Jews, but for all of us.

Did the Jews of the Old Testament come from what is now Israel? The answer is No.

"People who occupied some land two thousand years ago for a historically brief period, to the detriment of those who have been there since."

"Israel was established on the basis of theft. The State of Israel is Satan's offspring - a satanic offspring. It was founded on theft from the first moment. It was founded on the basis of robbery, terror, killing, torture, assassination, death, stealing land and killing people and will continue this way, never able to exist because its birth was unnatural, a satanic offspring, and cannot exist among human beings... It cannot exist naturally, like other nations in this world."

"Our position is that even if the Zionist State [Israel] is the size of a postage stamp it has no right to exist. Occupied Palestine must be decolonized, decasualized and restored to the Palestinian people as a single sovereign state. In plain English, the Zionist State must be dismantled."

"All Palestine should be returned to the Palestinians and other occupied lands should be returned to their owners. And the Zionist enterprise should cease to exist. Only then will the misery wrought by Zionism disappear."

This may take some people by surprise, but the UN has not used the term "Jewish state" since 1947. Resolution 181 then called for a "Jewish state" and an "Arab state," with gerrymandered borders designed to craft Jewish and Arab majorities in each state. But the attempt was rendered obsolete when Zionist forces established

"Israel" on a much greater swath of territory that had, in total, held a substantial Arab majority, and expelled most of the Arab residents. As refugees, according to the Geneva Conventions, those Arab residents have the right to return to their homes, villages, towns and cities. But their return would eliminate the Jewish majority in what became "Israel," so Israel hasn't allowed this.

Hence the UN cannot confirm Israel as a Jewish state (i.e., a state that can legitimately sustain a Jewish majority) without contradicting international law regarding the right of refugees. When the UN refers to "Israel" today, it does not understand Israel as the "Jewish state" in the old ethnic-majority terms of 1947, because Israel can be granted no "right" to an ethnic demography that would prevent the return of refugees.

Also, times have simply changed. In 1947, ethnic nationalism still made some belated sense, although it was already discredited by the dreadful abuses wreaked by Germany and Japan. Today, recognizing the "right" of any state to compose itself legally as an ethnic-majority state would clearly flout UN conventions on human rights and non-discrimination. The UN and EU therefore cannot openly endorse Israel's right to compose itself as one. It would make hash of international efforts in Rwanda, the Sudan, Kashmir, Afghanistan, Kosovo, and many other crisis spots.

So the US has lured the EU, Canada, and Norway into a trap. If they hold that Hamas must recognize Israel as a Jewish state (with a right to preserve an ethnic-Jewish majority), then they must state clearly that it endorses ethnic-majority governance. But those they cannot explicitly endorse Israel's right to ethno racy, because it would contradict international law as well as its own diplomacy in a host of other conflict zones, so on what grounds does they require Hamas to do so?

Why is the USA involved?
Due to (AIPAC), and a move for globalization, Israel and select Elites from USA will become the brokers of all Middle East Wealth.

Although the FBI seems to be keeping the two inquiries separate, there is strong circumstantial evidence that there was a behind-the-scenes connection between Chalabi and the Israelis. That is, the information circuit may have been in grown among the Neoconservatives, the Israelis and Chalabi's people.

It should be noted that Chalabi, the Neoconservatives, and Israel's Likud Party were allied in wanting to get up a US war against Iraq. But they were divided on the next stage, which was to get Washington to attack Iran, as well. Chalabi hates Saddam, but as an Iraqi Shiite has strong ties to Tehran, so he was not actually on board with Stage Two, and may have helped derail it, for which he is now hated in some Neoconservative circles.

ORGANIZED CRIME CONTROL MADE LEGAL??

NO TRUST LEFT, AMERICANS HAVE BEEN BURNT TOO MANY TIMES:

Why no TRUST? Well, it might have something to do with all the promises politicians have broken and prevarications they've committed. That sort of thing can get you a reputation, y'know. Atop that, Americans have good historical reasons to be suspicious of the motives of persons who seek power over them. The century just behind us was no testimonial to the morals or ethics of public officials. Recent history has heightened the sense among ordinary persons that most politicians and bureaucrats are up to no good. Thanks to the explosion of recording and communications technologies, we catch them with their hands in the cookie jar more often than ever before, which reinforces our cynicism about their innermost motives.

The 1986 amnesty bill was studded with promises of tightened border enforcement and improved immigration processes. None of them were kept. The recent Act of Congress mandating a fence along our border with Mexico was passed without a matching appropriation, making it impossible to implement.

It's about the trustworthiness of our elected officials and their less visible minions, who've contrived to evade the fulfillment of every promise they've made about immigration and border security for twenty-one years.

All the promises made by the Democrats, for the 110 th congresses. Have we seen any reform on campaigns, special interest groups, pork barrel spending, and any damn thing?

PLEASE name one fulfilled promise, where is there any reduction of corruption either side of the isle.

Have we seen any accountability, or any sincere demand for such from any congress member, senator or media source?

No one believes Iraq war is anything but an oil grab, with 655,000 + innocent civilians MURDERED. No one believes 911 investigations are complete. No one believes we are safer. No one agrees with our foreign policies toward Israel, we actually condemn their atrocities, but we the people are ignored.

WELL, wait until election time. We the American people are prepared.

Freedom of expression consists of the rights to freedom of speech, press, assembly and to petition the government for a redress of grievances.

A non-partisan, international foundation. Advocating free press and speech rights for all people has been under attack for the last six years.

Due to Presidential Executive Orders, the National Security Agency may have read this email without warning, warrant, or notice. They may do this without any judicial or legislative oversight. You have neither recourse nor protection save to call for the impeachment of the current President.

Many committees in the House and Senate, without taking any energy away from ending the war, can finally conduct the investigations that have gone undone for 6 years, exposing evidence that could very well lead to criminal, civil, or political accountability, as well as pressure to end the war and precedent to help prevent the next war.

State-Watch encourages the publication of investigative journalism and critical research in the fields of the state, civil liberties and openness, regarding telecommunications surveillance initiatives. State watch is a non-profit volunteer group comprised of lawyers, academics, journalists, researchers and community activists. The Global Internet Liberty Campaign is dedicated to promoting fundamental rights in the information society and cyberspace; towards that end, it has campaigned heavily against various government data retention proposals.

We're sorry, the page you're looking for has been moved or been deleted by order of your government. It is coming if our first Amendment rights are not protected.

Freedom of expression, speech, and press has been deluded down to. You have such right as long as it is Politically correct, does not offend the executive department, and conforms to its way of thinking. You are on my side or you will pay penalties for it. Penalties such as 112 Journalist killed, press offices being blown up. Shot at newly established check points, or fired if your information is somewhat incorrect. The rules from the executive: Influenced by lobbies, foreign or corporate, with no regard for the people. I notice, which I hope you have, the Media seems more willing to report and under less restraint the last couple of weeks. Like since the last election. The caution now remains with the "ownership of" and influence by outside lobbies, over mainstream media.

AMERICANS must remain vigilant, in protecting OUR Constitution. STAY INVOLVED...

OUR FEAR , IS FEAR OF THIS GOVERNMENT WHEN CONGRESS FAILS TO IMPEACH CRIMINALS

WHICH ACTION MAKES SENCE, IF ANY??

Black-Water gorillas torture experts given complete immunity in Iraq. But military people are prosecuted.

Border patrol agents jailed for doing their job. While drug smugglers go free.

Libby has a free pass after conviction. While CIA agents law suite, is thrown out of the Commander and Chief's appointed court.

Stay the course, while 3900 of our troops die in the middle of a civil WAR, over 650,000 civilians have been killed, 16,000,000 Iraqis displaced out of 28,000,000. No count on the thousands of troops & civilians injured.

Impeach all the war criminals and violators of our constitution, our laws, continue to commit perjury, and continue the course of deception to congress and the American people. That also ignores international laws, and UN resolutions. Withdraw all public funds from being used to support any religious State, religious monarchy.

International intervention by the United Nations

LT Col. USAF (RET) Robert Bowman....Say's 911 a inside JOB!! Say's Cheney main 911 suspects!!

The Former head of Star Wars missile defense program under President Ford and Carter has gone public to say the (GOVERNMENTS) official version of 911 is a Conspiracy theory and his main suspect for the architect of the attack is Vice President Dick Cheney.

Dr. Robert Bowman LT. COL. (USAF) Retired flew (101) Combat missions in Vietnam. He is the recipient of the Eisenhower Medal, The George F. Kennan Peace Prize, and The President's Medal of Veterans for Peace, the society of Military Engineers Gold Medal (TWICE), Siz Air Medals, and dozens of other awards and Honors as a PH.D is in Aeronautics and Nuclear Engineering from Caltech.

Bowman worked on the Star wars missile system for the US Government and has made a appearance on the Alex Jones Radio show and has evidence that the U.S. Government is not only lying about the events of 911 but is covering up of what really happened. LT. Col. Robert Bowman will be speaking in Chandler, Arizona this month at the 911 Accountability Conferences February 23-25, 2007 at the Crown Plaza in Chandler, Arizona.

For information on the 911 Accountability Conferences and LT. COL (USAF) Robert Bowman will also be speaking at this conference.

Website www.911Acountability.org or simply type in

911 Accountability conference Chandler, AZ
February 23-25, 2007

We all are aware that President George Bush believes in Santa Claus, The Easter Bunny, and the Tooth Fairy.

What will he believe when they all move to Dubai?

The Libby trial has provided a glimpse into the Cheney mob's operations, but it's hard to imagine that it will lead to an indictment of old Daddy War bucks himself.

No, if I had to bet on any investigation that could come back and bite him in the ass, it might be the Halliburton Nigeria bribery case.

The crimes of this gruesome creature will be documented in detail for at the least the first part of the 21st century. The MSM must bear responsibility for enabling the many war and corporate crimes perpetrated by this gang of war criminals. History has a very long memory and the truth will always out weigh spin and lies in its documentation.

War profiteering should be seen for the heinous crime that it is, and the fact that it's gone on for so long points a damning finger at a lot of people all the way back down the road. Patronage, bribery, and so forth, nothing happens in a vacuum, and 'business as usual' was the slogan that was used for years and years to describe goings-on in Washington,
and it's part of the reason that our country's so far into possibly even irrecoverable debt is due to the machinations of people like this.

Just remember that the Bush administration just replaced a number of top level federal prosecutors with lapdogs. Anyone want to guess who will be prosecuting any case against tricky Dick?

Halliburton paid $4 million to politicians for 600% gain on contracts since 2000
26 Sept., 2006
WASHINGTON, Sept. 26 (HalliburtonWatch.org) -- Halliburton spent $4.6 million since 2000 buying influence in Washington via campaign donations and lobbying, a HalliburtonWatch analysis reveals.

The board of directors and their spouses personally gave $828,701 to candidates for Congress and the presidency while Halliburton's political action committees gave $1.2 million, most of it donated to Republicans and political organizations with strong Republican ties.

The company spent an additional $2.6 million lobbying members of Congress, the White House and federal agencies.

Conclusion: Halliburton's $4.6 million in political arm-twisting since 2000 has paid-off magnificently as the company's government contracts ballooned by over 600 percent in value by the end of 2005, mostly because of the war in Iraq.

In 2000, Halliburton was the 20th largest federal contractor, receiving $763 million in federal contracts. By 2005, Halliburton had grown to become the 6th largest federal contractor, receiving nearly $6 billion in federal contracts during that year.

Between March 2003 and June 30, 2006, Halliburton received $18.5 billion in revenue from the federal government for the war in Iraq.

The company has seen its profits in government contracting almost quadruple to $330 million in 2005 compared to $84 million in 2004.

During one quarter in 2005, Halliburton's war profits skyrocketed by 284 percent.

War contracts, intensified violence in the Middle East and record oil prices helped quadruple the stock price between the March 2003 invasion of Iraq and March 2006. As a result, the board of directors together saw the value of their stock holdings in the company increase by over $100 million.

CEO David Lesar holds the largest number of shares of any Halliburton official, owning 844,928 common shares and share options as of March 1, 2006. The shares were worth $17.3 million as the troops first rolled into Baghdad in 2003. Three years later, on April 10, 2006, the shares were worth $66.8 million, for a $49.5

million gain. Lesar sold an additional 631,071 shares during the war at various stock prices for gross amounts totaling between $12.9 million on March 20, 2003, and $49.9 million on March 1, 2006.

Did a Democratic member of Congress improperly enlist the support of a major pro-Israel lobbying group to try to win a top committee assignment? That's the question at the heart of an ongoing investigation by the FBI and Justice Department prosecutors, who are examining whether Rep. Jane Harman of California and the American Israel Public Affairs Committee (AIPAC) may have violated the law in a scheme to get Harman reappointed as the top Democrat on the House intelligence committee, according to knowledgeable sources in and out of the U.S. government.

The sources tell TIME that the investigation by Justice and the Federal Bureau of Investigation, which has simmered out of sight since about the middle of last year, is examining whether Harman and AIPAC arranged for wealthy supporters to lobby House Democratic leader Nancy Pelosi on Harman's behalf.

Ring-around-the Rosie, it is well know that Santa has been working both sides of the isle for years.

AIPAC is the leading player in what is sometimes referred to as "The Israel Lobby"--a coalition that includes major Jewish groups, neoconservative intellectuals and Christian Zionists. With its impressive contacts among Hill staffers, influential grassroots supporters and deep connections to wealthy donors, AIPAC is the lobby's key emissary to Congress. But in many ways, AIPAC has become greater than just another lobby; its work has made unconditional support for Israel an accepted cost of doing business inside the halls of Congress. AIPAC's interest, Israel's interest and America's interest are today perceived by most elected leaders to be one and the same. Christian conservatives increasingly aligned with AIPAC demand unwavering support for Israel from their Republican leaders. (In mid-July, 3,000-plus evangelicals came to town for the first annual "Christian United for Israel" summit.) And

Democrats are equally concerned about alienating Jewish voters and Jewish donors--long a cornerstone of their party. Some in Congress are deeply uncomfortable with AIPAC's militant worldview and heavy-handed tactics, but most dare not say so publicly.

Do you believe there has been a point at any other time in history that the quality and capacity of those serving in the executive, legislative and judicial branches has ever been lower?

Yes   5% 480 votes

No   95% 9088 votes
Total: 9568 votes

WE AMERICANS FEAR THIS USA GOVERNMENT AND ADMINISTRATION "MORE" THEN WE DO AL-QAEDA. (AN ORGANIZATION CREATED TO RESIST THE FOREIGN POLICIES BASED ON ISRAELI INTEREST, NOT AMERICA'S.)

AMERICAN VOTERS PRESSURE YOUR REPRESENTATIVES

CONGRESS HAS BEEN REDUCED TO WALLPAPER

AMERICAN voters need to pressure THEIR REPRESENTATIVES: THE PEOPLES REPRESENTATIVES who say they favor "benchmarks," but have consistently opposed efforts to set a deadline for troop withdrawal. They voted against every timeline bill, and voted to continue funding the war with no restrictions on the money. The House will vote again on the war in Iraq in September, and all elected officials need to hear the opposition to the war every day until then.

The struggle to end the war is intensifying; please take some time to help us reach one of the most important battlegrounds.

The Bush administration is determined to veto any bill that mandates a withdrawal of troops, and as of now there are not enough votes to override his veto.

The only thing this surge will accomplish is a surge of more death and destruction.

Ever since a new Congress got elected last November, we've been waiting for it to end the violations of the Constitution and the lawless behavior of the Bush administration.

It's gone from bad to intolerable. And we must let Congressional leaders know -- in no uncertain terms -- that it's time to start standing tall and stop caving in.

When our leaders behave like sheep, their constituents need to know it. That's why we are going to run an ad in Nancy Pelosi's and Harry Reid's hometown newspapers.

Bush has crippled checks and balances and protections against government abuses. If these claims and practices are not repudiated, the precedents will lie around like loaded weapons, ready for use by any White House incumbent to intimidate rivals or to destroy the rule of law.

The president has reduced Congress to wallpaper. He has asserted executive privilege to foil the congressional power of investigation - the most important because sunshine is the best disinfectant for lawlessness.

We also need fair taxation:

NATIONAL DEBT IS NOW: $9,686,542,446,617.56

THOSE RESPONCIPLE AND INVOLVED SHALL NOW PAY THEIR SHARE.

William H. Rehnquist spoke for the court:
Both tax exemptions and tax deductibility are a form of subsidy that is administered through the tax system. A tax exemption has much the same effect as cash grant to the organization of the amount of tax it would have to pay on its income.

The significance of this decision is often overlooked. If tax exemption is a form of subsidy, then church property tax exemption is a clear violation of the establishment clause of the First Amendment. All that is necessary to make church property tax exemption a thing of the past is for an irate taxpayer who is tired of high taxes to file suit to force churches to pay their "fair share."

Tenth Circuit Court addressed, and held that "tax exemption is a privilege, a matter of grace rather than a right."

The question of tax exemption for churches is clear: the foundation has been laid for taxing church property and perhaps even church income.

As the budget deficits of the federal, state and local government's increase, the possibility of taxing church property also rises -- despite the long history of tax exemption.

We are sick and tired of the "Zionist-Movement" the cost of the "WAR" they demanded, the amount of holdings & investments rather then any amount of return to the community. The threat of Falwell to use 200,000 preachers to preach his message from the pulpit is not only wrong it is unlimited use of propaganda!

The millions spent on foolish campaigns designed to shape or change public opinion in regard to this or that: divorce, birth control, the falseness of the Darwinian theory, or almost anything in connection with science and history! The blather about saints and cures and bringing all to Jesus, the while taxes are evaded and the scummy politicians whom they endorse, or even nominate and elect to office, proceed to rob the public in favor of the corporations and churches whom they serve! No wonder ignorance, no wonder illusion, when those with power in the religious field knowingly delude and mislead the masses! The things told them! That it is important to vote for this or that crook; uphold religion; it is good for the people to go to war, to put religion in the schools, to give into the hands of these mental bandits the care and education of all children, so that they may be properly enslaved by religion! (A slave, in my opinion, is the man who does not think for himself. A man with knowledge is not powerless.) But always with suave and polished words.
How about a Robertson or Bush Whisper! God has told me, and I will tell you, and you shall follow and sustain me as my servant who am the servant of God! SURE!

One would think from that that the Churches were a branch of the Government, a public institution, whereas they are only semipublic, being under the control of a special group of patrons, and as such should be taxed and made to pay the same as any other self-aggrandizing corporation.

The State now should not permit them to go tax free, and should, should it not? Enjoy and participate in any money-making of this nature, which is certainly no legitimate function of religion. Then look close at the MONEY!!

Well now, church buildings alone in America, without parsonages, investments,securities,schools,orphanages,hospitals and monasteries, are valued in the trillions. Investments such as in Defense etc, also will be in the trillions. Do they ever cough up in crisis,

No they just manage the money from the congregation they solicit it from. Let's call it Alms instead of Tyethings. America now represented by the money-mad leaders who are dictating not only the economics but the philosophy of the country and using the religionists to help them. Or might it be the fool led by fools.

We will sue for tax fairness due to the last six years of Church involvement in Politics, openly judging people with a different political view, telling a congregation they must support the republican party, and support an unjust "WAR".

Now pay for it, I left the Church because I'm proud to be a Democrat, American, a Christian, but no longer a member of any denomination that supports corruption and/or WAR. BLAME THE PAT ROBERTSONS AND JERRY FALWELLS FOR INVOLVING CHURCH & STATE.

I pay Taxes for your injustice, now you will also.

I REQUEST THE ACLU TO TAKE UP SUCH ISSUE FOR THE BENEFIT OF ALL THOSE PAYING SUCH COST!!

A question that will never occur to the American public because, so long as America's mainstream media, Congress and president maintain their pact of silence, few Americans will ever know the true cost of Israel to U.S. taxpayers.

There are immense political and military costs to the U.S. for its consistent support of Israel during Israel's half-century of disputes with the Palestinians and all of its Arab neighbors.

Only rarely is a critical word uttered among politicians regarding AIPAC and its associates that support unjust and aggressive (and disastrous) U.S. policies toward the peoples of the Middle East. We aim to change that.

For too long, policies that support Israeli militarism and occupation have gone unchallenged. Political voices raising even minor disagreements with prevailing policies are silenced or subject to campaigns of intimidation. We must open the door to full debate regarding U.S. relationship with Israel and U.S. policy with other countries in the region.

Horrific acts of violence and deadly attacks on innocent people, carried out by the Israeli military.
In defiance of the American people's wishes, and the World in general, when push comes to shove the U.S. government manages to support a hostile Jewish State. The message is also delivered from the pulpit with vigor, when in reality Israel is against Christianity. Worse yet, through their greed for   money, we have sold or gifted this hostile nation, (Nuclear, Biological and Chemical) weapons with the missiles to deliver them. These weapons now threaten the world.

Look how the USA has equipped Israeli military better than our own reserve & National Guard units.

NO matter what rhetoric our government states, the facts are before us all, IF you take the time to research it.

According to this administration they are never wrong. All disseminated policies are infallible and morally justified up to and including torture and the victimization of entire populations. According to this administration the home front is perfect, there are plenty of jobs to spare, massive budget deficits are good for the country, rising poverty indicators aren't important, more uninsured individuals aren't anything to worry about, illegal immigrants who are taking away jobs and driving down labor dollars in addition to draining social service needs is a healthy part of a thriving nation, corporate off shoring is good for the economy etc etc etc.

Everything that is bad for this country as a whole is deemed good by this administration up to an including wars, the destruction of the social service safety network that is designed to protect all US citizens, reduction in labors dollars even as inflation indexes which do not include basic consumables like food, rise. These are examples of crazy making at its finest. Do not believe what you see and experience as an individual only believe the propaganda that I set before you as your leader.

Hmmm-So maybe this letter isn't really directed to you at all Mr. President. Maybe its audience needs to be the American people, the ones who are going to have to, (or may already have); paid dearly for the policy you and yours (the corporations and your advisors) have already advanced and acted upon. Maybe they need to be encouraged to read and study the effects of your disastrous domestic and foreign policies. Maybe they need to step outside of themselves and their immediate needs and recognize that we as American citizens are all in this together whether we be Republicans, Democrats, Independents, or other affiliated parties, and that we collectively on both the home and international front will be paying for the disastrous results of your administration for a long time to come.

This country needs you to, through word and deed; re-establish the greatness that was once the United States of America. That greatness began with dialogue and the recognition of common cause by and between all people. Fail to restore the checks and balances and you will do so at your own peril.

Our leaders in Congress need to know that Gonzales' resignation doesn't wipe away this Administration's ongoing abuses of power and it certainly doesn't excuse its rubber-stamping of the Bush administration's illegal wiretapping program.

While the departure of one of the worst attorneys general in our nation's history certainly gives us something to celebrate, we cannot rest for even a minute.

We cannot let Harry Reid or Nancy Pelosi think for one second that now that Alberto Gonzales has resigned we will quietly fade away. If anything, we need to speak up even louder against a president who has violated the Constitution and the leaders in Congress who let him get away with it.

If lawmakers don't act with clarity and conviction in the weeks ahead, this Congress, headed by House Speaker Nancy Pelosi and Senate Leader Harry Reid, will be remembered as the Congress that failed freedom. We can't let that happen.

Each and every one of us must remain outspoken and vigilant. It's going to be a fight to get this Congress to conduct real oversight and restore our Constitution. But with your help, we can get it done.

STOP MAD COWBOY DISEASE:

WHY WE HAVE BECOME HATED & WHY WE WILL NOT WIN!!

If any citizen were to make a statement recommending assassination, we would be picked up and thrown into a jail, or sent to guantanamo bay.

Why is it? A complete out of his mind jerk like this raving maniac PAT ROBERTSON, can go around recommending an assassination, foretelling the future, stating GOD told him about an attack is coming. We know he is not out of step with the White-House, but shouldn't he also face criminal charges like anyone else would? At least put him in an institution.

OF COURSE WE ALL KNOW THERE IS A LIST A MILE LONG OF "ZIONIST" THAT BELONG LOCKED UP..

The Rev. Jerry Falwell said that he and several leaders of the Southern Baptist Convention would mobilize evangelical churches to oppose steps to give up any more territory to the Palestinians.

To get out the word on Israel, Falwell said, "There are about 200,000 evangelical pastors in America, and we're asking them all through e-mail, faxes, letters, telephone, to go into their pulpits and use their influence in support of the state of Israel and the prime minister." Which any one, attending a Church knows they have done so. Political messages from most every pulpit across our nation in support of the republican party, president Bush policy, and in complete support of the WAR for Israel's interest not Americas.. Now pay taxes on all tax free property.

This comes at a time when Israel is under pressure from both the World (UN) and some American Jewish groups to break an impasse in the peace efforts.

Democrats in Congress have moved quickly - and commendably - to strengthen ethics rules. But truly groundbreaking reform was prevented, in part, because of the efforts of the pro-Israel lobby to preserve one of its most critical functions: taking members of Congress on free "educational" trips to Israel.

The pro-Israel lobby does most of its work without publicity. But every member of Congress and every would-be candidate for Congress comes to quickly understand a basic lesson. Money needed to run for office can come with great ease from supporters of Israel, provided that the candidate makes certain promises, in writing, to vote favorably on issues considered important to Israel. What drives much of congressional support for Israel is fear - fear that the pro-

Israel lobby will either withhold campaign contributions or give money to one's opponent.

Pro-Israel groups worked vigorously to ensure that the new reforms would allow them to keep hosting members of Congress on trips to Israel. According to the Jewish Daily Forward newspaper, congressional filings show Israel as the top foreign destination for privately sponsored trips. Nearly 10 percent of overseas congressional trips taken between 2000 and 2005 were to Israel. Most are paid for by the American Israel Education Foundation, a sister organization of the American Israel Public Affairs Committee, the major pro-Israel lobby group.

New rules require all trips to be pre-approved by the House Ethics Committee, but Rep. Barney Frank (D) of Massachusetts says this setup will guarantee that tours of Israel continue. Ron Kampeas of the Jewish Telegraphic Agency reported consensus among Jewish groups that "the new legislation would be an inconvenience, but wouldn't seriously hamper the trips to Israel that are considered a critical component of congressional support for Israel."

What the pro-Israel lobby reaps for its investment in these tours is congressional support for Israeli desires. For years, Israel has relied on billions of dollars in US taxpayer money. Shutting off this government funding would seriously impair Israel's harsh occupation.

One wonders what policies Congress might support toward Israel and the Palestinians absent the distorting influence of these Israel trips - or if more members toured Palestinian lands. America sent troops to Europe to prevent the killing of civilians in the former Yugoslavia. But when it comes to flagrant human rights violations committed by Israel, the US sends more money and shields Israel from criticism.

Congress regularly passes resolutions lauding Israel, even when its actions are deplorable, providing it political cover. Meanwhile, polls suggest most Americans want the Bush administration to steer a middle course in working for peace between Israelis and the Palestinians.

Consider, too, how the Israel lobby twists US foreign policy into a dangerous double standard regarding nuclear issues. The US rattles its sabers at Iran for its nuclear energy ambitions - and alleged pursuit of nuclear arms - while remaining silent about Israel's nuclear-weapons arsenal.

Members of Congress may not be aware just how damaging their automatic support for Israel is to America's interest. At a minimum, US policies toward Israel have cost it valuable allies in the Middle East and other parts of the Muslim world.

If Congress is serious about ethics reform, it should not protect the Israel lobby from the consequences. A totally taxpayer-funded travel budget for members to take foreign fact-finding trips, with authorization to be made by committee heads, would be an important first step toward a foreign policy that genuinely serves America.

FAIR TAX

THE END OF DEMOCRACY, AND OUR CONSTITUTION:
THERE IS NO PLACE FOR POLITICS IN GOD'S HOUSE:
MINISTERS OR POILITICIANS IN THE PULPIT:

Can you believe it. The republicans still will tell you, God told them to kill more people in the world then what will vote for them in any coming election. To profit from WAR, and give the Church invest. in more WAR equipment. To assist Israel in their genocide of Palestinians, and to ignore the suffering in Sudan. To create more and more widows, orphans, and disabled people so the drug companies can sell more goodies. Paid for by the middle class tax payer, certainly nothing from the Church, except in alms from the poor congregations. I certainly hope that the Christian people don't fall for the deceptions of the Republican party again. I hope they realize what separation of church & state means. I hope they pay attention and stay home praying for change in the world. Listen to their GOD tell them not to concern themselves with the business of government and corruption. It will always demoralize its people.

Where in your BIBLE does it say to involve yourselves in Caesar's business.

Where does it say you should not pay taxes, and should invest your funds in WAR.?

NO MORE PUBLIC FUNDS, TAX DOLLARS, FOR ISRAEL SUPPORT!
We as citizens of the United States request that no further funding of a religious state with Our public funds continue. We request that no further military aid be given to a religious state. We also request a return of our funds. From the, "Jewish State of Israel".

Our constitution specifically separates church & state. NONE of our tax dollars should be used in support of any religious institution, government or
annex of such state.

They may have declared themselves a separate State, but our constitution strictly forbids using our public money or tax dollars from supporting such, and we demand that such practice discontinue immediately.

OXYMORONS:

DEMOCRACY----BUSH REGIME
OCCUPYING-----LIBERATE
CHRISTIAN-------REPUBLICAN
ETHICS -----------CARL ROVE

Fourteen Characteristics of Fascism:

1. Powerful and Continuing Nationalism - Fascist regimes tend to make constant use of patriotic mottos, slogans, symbols, songs, and other paraphernalia. Flags are seen everywhere, as are flag symbols on clothing and in public displays.
2. Disdain for the Recognition of Human Rights - Because of fear of enemies and the need for security, the people in fascist regimes are persuaded that human rights can be ignored in certain cases because of "need." The people tend to look the other way or even approve of torture, summary executions, assassinations, long incarcerations of prisoners, etc.
3. Identification of Enemies/Scapegoats as a Unifying Cause - The people are rallied into a unifying patriotic frenzy over the need to eliminate a perceived common threat or foe: racial, ethnic or religious minorities; liberals; communists; socialists, terrorists, etc.
4. Supremacy of the Military - Even when there are widespread domestic problems the military is given a disproportionate amount of government funding, and the domestic agenda is neglected, Soldiers and military service are glamorized.

5. Rampant Sexism - The governments of fascist nations tend to be almost exclusively male-dominated. Under fascist regimes, traditional gender roles are made more rigid. Divorce, abortion and homosexuality are suppressed and the state is represented as the ultimate guardian of the family institution.

6. Controlled Mass Media - Sometimes to media is directly controlled by the government, but in other cases, the media is indirectly controlled by government regulation, or sympathetic media spokespeople and executives. Censorship, especially in war time, is very common.

7. Obsession with National Security - Fear is used as a motivational tool by the government over the masses.

8. Religion and Government are intertwined - Governments in fascist nations tend to use the most common religion in the nation as a tool to manipulate public opinion. Religious rhetoric and terminology is common from government leaders, even when the major tenets of the religion are diametrically opposed to the government's policies or actions.

9. Corporate Power is protected - The industrial and business aristocracy of a fascist nation often is the ones who put the government leaders into power, creating a mutually beneficial business/government relationship and power elite.

10. Labor Power is suppressed - Because the organizing power of labor is the only real threat to a fascist government, labor unions are either eliminated entirely, or are severely suppressed.

11. Disdain for Intellectuals and the Arts - Fascist nations tend to promote and tolerate open hostility to higher education, and academia. It is not uncommon for professors and other academics to be censored or even arrested. Free expression in the arts and letters is openly attacked.

12. Obsession with Crime and Punishment - Under fascist regimes, the police are given almost limitless power to enforce laws. The people are often willing to overlook police abuses and even forego civil liberties in the name of patriotism. There is often a national police force with virtually unlimited power in fascist nations.

13. Rampant Cronyism and Corruption - Fascist regimes almost always are governed by groups of friends and associates who appoint

each other to government positions and use governmental power and authority to protect their friends from accountability. It is not uncommon in fascist regimes for national resources and even treasures to be appropriated or even outright stolen by government leaders.

14. Fraudulent Elections - Sometimes elections in fascist nations are a complete sham. Other times elections are manipulated by smear campaigns against or even assassination of opposition candidates, use of legislation to control voting numbers or political district boundaries, and manipulation of the media. Fascist nations also typically use their judiciaries to manipulate or control elections.

WE HAVE WITNESSED ALL 14 OVER THE LAST SEVEN YEARS.

THE CONTROLLED ELECTRONIC VOTING WILL BE THE LAST, AND END TO DEMOCRACY AND OUR CONSTITUTION.

"Fascism should more appropriately be called Corporatism because it is a merger of State and corporate power."

"Fascism is coming to America in the name of national security."

The above fourteen point definition of fascism clearly describes the current state of the United States of America, particularly under the second Bush Administration - a regime awash in corruption, secrecy, theocracy, and militarism and election fraud. Never before in the history of this country have the people as a whole been rendered so powerless by a ruling, corporate, elite and gang of "Project For a New Century" imperialists.

Given the media control by a handful of powerful and unelected few, never before has the need for radical reforms been so necessary, and yet so difficult to mount.

It is very apparent, that the Fascism-anti-Christ has taken over the Christians already.

WE WANT CONTRACTS FOR EACH ELECTED OFFICIAL. KEEP YOUR PROMISES OR LEAVE.

NO MORE PUBLIC FUNDS, TAX DOLLARS, FOR ISRAEL SUPPORT!

We as citizens of the United States request that no further funding of a religious state with Our public funds continue. We request that no further military aid be given to a religious state. We also request a return of our funds. From the:"Jewish State of Israel". Our constitution specifically separates church & state. NONE of our tax dollars should be used in support of any religious institution, government or annex of such state.

They may have declared themselves a separate State, but our constitution strictly forbids using our public money or tax dollars from supporting such, and we demand that such practice discontinue immediately

IT SEEMS LIKE BUSINESS AS USUAL, NOTHING CHANGES, NO MATTER ABOUT THE PEOPLES DEMANDS.JUST MORE & MORE DECEPTION.

TO Columnist Tom Delay:
(King of Special interest, crime bosses, campaign funding from lobbyist, and War profiteering) Lobbyist synonymous with bribery. Government in DC-synonymous with lobbyist.

We certainly know now that Republicans in power cannot be trusted with the Constitution or the Budget. OR ANYTHING FOR THAT MATTER:
Twice now they just found it easier to go off and make wars rather than tackle the real reforms America needs. Don't forget that Bush Father also caved in on taxes & spending, once he started his war, just as his son followed the same path. The warfare state always pays homage to the Welfare State.

The Republican motto right now: Bomb, Bomb, Bomb, Bomb, bomb Iran.
War songs seem to be their national Anthem.

Freedom of expression consists of the rights to freedom of speech, press, assembly and to petition the government for a redress of grievances.

A nonpartisan, international foundation advocating free press and speech rights for all people Has been under attack for the last six years.

Due to Presidential Executive Orders, the National Security Agency may have read this email without warning, warrant, or notice. They may do this without any judicial or legislative oversight. You have neither recourse nor protection save to call for the impeachment of the current President.

Many committees in the House and Senate, without taking any energy away from ending the war, can finally conduct the investigations that have gone undone for 6 years, exposing evidence that could very well lead to criminal, civil, or political accountability, as well as pressure to end the war and precedent to help prevent the next war.

State-Watch encourages the publication of investigative journalism and critical research in the fields of the state, civil liberties and openness, regarding telecommunications surveillance initiatives. State watch is a non-profit volunteer group comprised of lawyers, academics, journalists, researchers and community activists. The Global Internet Liberty Campaign is dedicated to promoting fundamental rights in the information society and cyberspace; towards that end, it has campaigned heavily against various government data retention proposals.

Freedom of expression, speech, and press has been deluded down to. You have such right as long as it is Politically correct, does not offend the executive department, and conforms to its way of thinking. You are on my side or you will pay penalties for it. Penalties such as 112 Journalist killed, press offices being blown up. Shot at newly established check points, or fired if your information is somewhat incorrect.

AMERICANS must remain vigilant, in protecting OUR Constitution. STAY INVOLVED...

Contact the Media about Impeachment Coverage.

 Bush Administration has ignored the Constitution. Impeachable offenses need to be investigated. These are two statements that are true, yet are rarely heard via the mainstream American media. We have all seen what complacency in the media can bring. The Iraq War could not have been executed without it. Impeachment is being framed as a distraction or as revenge. It is time for the media to discuss the real evidence that supports Impeachment and leave the opining to the citizens of this country.

Bush/Cheney Have Disgraced Their Office:

Bush and Cheney had plunged the nation into war "under false pretenses." Exploiting the public trust in the Presidency, Bush had persuaded, over the uncritical mass media, day after day, before the war, a majority of the American people that Saddam Hussein possessed chemical, biological weapons and nuclear weapons programs, was connected to al-Qaeda and 9/11 and was a threat to the United States.

The case for impeachment is so strong that, recently, hardly a day goes by without more disclosures which strengthen any number of impeachable offenses that could form a Congressional action under our Constitution. An illegal war, to begin with, against our Constitution which says only Congress can declare war. An illegal war under domestic laws, and international law, and conducted illegally under international conventions to which the US belongs, should cause an outcry against this small clique of outlaws committing war crimes who have hijacked our national government.

By any legal standard and by the requirements of the U.S. Constitution (Article 1, Section 8, the war-declaring authority), George W. Bush and Dick Cheney are probably the most impeachable President and Vice President in American history.

What matters is that impeachment in this case - based on the authority of Congress to charge the President and Vice President with "high crimes and misdemeanors" - is a patriotic cause rooted in the wisdom of our founding fathers who did not want another King George III in the guise of a President.

Both George W. Bush and Dick Cheney should resign. They have disgraced their office and bled the nation. They have shattered the public trust in so many serious ways that will only become worse in the coming months. Not only America's, but the entire international communities trust.

The "huge challenge" the Bush administration faces in trouble spots around the world. What takes place in Afghanistan, Egypt, Iran, Libya, Morocco, Pakistan, Saudi Arabia, Syria, Turkey and especially the Israeli-Palestinian relationship may well be as significant for the Middle East as what occurs in Iraq.

What happens in China, India, Russia, Europe and Africa may well be as important for the future of the international system as what transpires in the Middle East.

Diplomacy -- the oldest tool in international relations -- seems fated for revival. The people chosen to share leadership in the State Department and to represent the United States abroad must be skilled diplomats and not just Bush loyalists.

Hypocrisy--Two nations stand out above all others as notorious serial abusers of UN resolutions - the US and Israel. Over the last half century, the US has used its Security Council veto many dozens of times to prevent any resolutions from passing condemning Israel for its abusive or hostile actions or that were inimical to Israeli interests. The State of Israel was established in 1948. Ever since, there has been continuous violence between Jews and Arabs in Israel, and between Israel and its neighbors. Always Israel is the aggressor, occupier, and most importantly, transgressor of GODS LAWS. The fact of Bush/Cheney administrations loyalty to Israel, Diplomats should be chosen very carefully, and should be persons with integrity and ethics Trustworthy. The most experienced such as past Presidents Carter & Clinton.

Ten Reasons to Impeach George Bush and Dick Cheney

I ask Congress to impeach President Bush and Vice President Cheney for the following reasons:

1. Violating the United Nations Charter by launching an illegal "War of Aggression" against Iraq without cause, using fraud to sell the war to Congress and the public, misusing government funds to begin bombing without Congressional authorization, and subjecting our military personnel to unnecessary harm, debilitating injuries, and deaths.

2. Violating U.S. and international law by authorizing the torture of thousands of captives, resulting in dozens of deaths, and keeping prisoners hidden from the International Committee of the Red Cross.

3. Violating the Constitution by arbitrarily detaining Americans, legal residents, and non-Americans, without due process, without charge, and without access to counsel.

4. Violating the Geneva Conventions by targeting civilians, journalists, hospitals, and ambulances, and using illegal weapons, including white phosphorous, depleted uranium, and a new type of napalm.

5. Violating U.S. law and the Constitution through widespread wiretapping of the phone calls and emails of Americans without a warrant.

6. Violating the Constitution by using "signing statements" to defy hundreds of laws passed by Congress.

7. Violating U.S. and state law by obstructing honest elections in 2000, 2002, 2004, and 2006.

8. Violating U.S. law by using paid propaganda and disinformation, selectively and misleadingly leaking classified information, and exposing the identity of a covert CIA operative working on sensitive WMD proliferation for political retribution.

9. Subverting the Constitution and abusing Presidential power by asserting a "Unitary Executive Theory" giving unlimited powers to the President, by obstructing efforts by Congress and the Courts to review and restrict Presidential actions, and by promoting and signing legislation negating the Bill of Rights and the Writ of Habeas Corpus.

10. Gross negligence in failing to assist New Orleans residents after Hurricane Katrina, in ignoring urgent warnings of an Al Qaeda attack prior to Sept. 11, 2001, and in increasing air pollution causing global warming.

Israel held fast to its policy of ambiguity concerning its nuclear weapons program after the incoming U.S. Defense Secretary Robert Gates said that the Jewish state possesses an atomic bomb.

In his confirmation hearing before the Senate, Robert Gates reiterated U.S. claims that Iran's atomic program isn't peaceful, but explained Tehran's motivation to acquire nuclear weapons.

"They are surrounded by powers with nuclear weapons — Pakistan to their east, the Russians to the north, the Israelis to the west and us in the Persian Gulf," he told the Senate committee on Wednesday.

Although Israel is believed to be the only nuclear-armed country in the Middle East – with a nuclear arsenal of at least 200 warheads -- it maintains a policy of ambiguity on the issue, neither admitting nor denying that it does posses atomic arms.

Commenting on Gates' remarks, Israeli government spokesman Miri Eisin said: "There is no direct Israeli comment".

Israeli experts also played down the importance of the comments.

How do you view the Iranian President's letter to Americans?
RESULTS:

Sign of willingness to engage Washington
(54 %)

Propaganda stunt
(46 %)

Do you believe President Bush's actions justify impeachment? *
386005 responses

Yes, between the secret spying, the deceptions leading to war and more, there is plenty to justify putting him on trial.
87%

No, like any president, he has made a few missteps, but nothing approaching "high crimes and misdemeanors."
4.5%

No, the man has done absolutely nothing wrong. Impeachment would just be a political lynching.
6.4%

I don't know.
1.9%

IMPEACHMENT WILL HAVE TO COME ABOUT. HE REFUSES TO COMPLY WITH THE WISHES OF THE AMERICAN PEOPLE, BOWS TO ISRAEL & AIPAC, CONTINUES ON A STAY THE COURSE AGENDA.

DIPLOMACY: NOT MORE WAR, KILLING, AND OCCUPATIONS.

THE LAST BIG DITCH EFFORT, AS THEY WILL CALL IT.
IT SEEMS obvious, doesn't it? If America cannot bring peace to Iraq, it should get out. Everyone now agrees that the old policy of "staying the course" will not work, so the debate in Washington today is between those who believe that some other strategy might work and should be tried, and those who think that nothing will, so America should get out now.

The White House delay prompted criticism from Democratic congressional leaders and from at least one Republican senator, Chuck Hagel, who said President Bush was failing to show sufficient urgency about Iraq despite months of escalating violence.

BUSH: We will stay the course; we will complete the job in Iraq.
BUSH: And so the United States of America will stay the course and we will complete the task. We'll help Iraq develop a democracy and the world will be better off for it. We're making steady progress.

A free Iraq will mean a peaceful world. And it's very important for us to stay the course, and we will stay the course.

Nothing like this surprises us anymore. They know they can get away with this crap, so why not. Its all fun and games until 655,000 Iraqis are dead. Then its just fun... for Bush/Cheney, Israel, Mossad, and AIPAC, do they call it a "Justified Genocide".

What, are you "cutting and running" from "stay the course" now?

Bush was for stay the course, before he was against it.

I think he deliberately lies just so he can get caught at it. That's one twisted individual.

Political scientists John Mearsheimer (U of Chicago) and Stephen Walt (Harvard) bravely take on the issue of the pro-Israel lobby in Washington and the way it distorts US foreign policy in the Middle East. Most American Jews deeply disagree with the policies advocated by the American Enterprise Institute, the Jewish Institute for National Security Affairs, etc., but a sliver of the political spectrum, falsely insisting that it represents all American Jews, manages to skew US politics and reporting on the issue of Palestine.

Anyone following the current situation in the Palestinian/Israeli relationship can clearly see that the Palestinians are boxed into a corner from which they cannot escape to construct a viable country.

With all the billions going to Israel for which no accounting is requested, then surely millions are cycled back to the US to corrupt Congress, look at the construction going on in Israel. Look close at the no bid contracts, and the Secret projects.

I wonder if anyone has been looking into the backwash of cash.

NOW LETS GET REAL: The deal going on is the permanent bases in the Middle East "IRAQ-PLAN" as Chalibi described, the connection to Israel's new base. Paid for, with swindled American funds, Electronic control and surveillance equipment spying on Israel's neighbors. WHY??

We need to cut the funding. No appropriations for any more WAR, Building etc. (NOTHING WITH OUT OVER SIGHT).

THANK JIMMY CARTER FOR WRITING THE TRUTH IMPEACHMENT IS NECESSARY TO CHANGE COURSE!!

Carter defends criticism of Israel

Jimmy Carter, the ex-US president, has defended his criticisms of Israeli policy in his latest book, saying he hopes to erode the "impenetrable wall" that stops Americans from seeing the true plight of the Palestinian people.

His book has been criticized by pro-Israeli groups and led to the resignation of Kenneth Stein, a Carter Centre fellow.

Carter said he hoped Palestine: Peace Not Apartheid would provoke a debate on Israeli policy.

Jewish groups have launched petitions criticizing Carter's use of the word "apartheid" - the system of racial separation once used in South Africa - to describe Israel's treatment of the Palestinians.

Carter said that debate had been stifled by the media and others.

"It's almost a universal silence concerning anything that might be critical of current policies of the Israeli government," he said.

"Worse than apartheid"

Carter said he stands by his use of the "apartheid" and cited the fences, electric sensors and concrete slabs that Israel has built in the West Bank as an example of the divide.

"It's almost a universal silence concerning anything that might be critical of current policies of the Israeli government."

Jimmy Carter, former US president
"I think its worse, in many ways, than apartheid in South Africa," Carter said.

The book follows the Israeli-Palestinian peace process, starting with Carter's 1977-1980 presidency and the Camp David peace accord he negotiated between Israel and Egypt.

It blames Israel, the Palestinians, the US and many others, but it is most critical of Israel.

Stein, an Emory University professor, sent a letter to Carter claiming the book was "one-sided" and "is not based on unvarnished analysis; it is replete with factual errors, copied materials not cited, superficialities, glaring omissions, and simply invented segments."

"Tremendous intimidation"

Carter said on Friday that Stein had not played a role in the Carter Centre in 13 years and that his post as a fellow was an honorary title.

He said: "When I decided to write this book, I didn't even think about involving Ken, from ancient times, to come in and help."

He added that the book had been vetted by Carter Centre staff and an unnamed "distinguished" reporter.

Carter, who won the Nobel Peace Prize in 2002, lamented the lack of discussion of Israeli policy in the US.

"There's a tremendous intimidation in this country that has silenced our people. And it's not just individuals; it's not just folks who are running for office. It's the news media as well," he said.

Carter, who has led efforts to monitor several elections in the Palestinian Territories since leaving office, said bringing peace to the Middle East is the most important commitment in his public life.

EXPRESS WHAT THE "MANDATE" IS:

WE WANT NEW LEADERSHIP IN A NEW DIRECTION.

AMERICA FOR AMERICANS:

WHO IS TO BLAME FOR FAILURE, WHICH WILL CONTINUE TO BE A FAILURE WHAT SHOULD WE HAVE LEARNED LONG AGO??

ISRAEL'S GOOD NEIGHBOR POLICIES:

The carnage, left by Israel, "creates the desire for revenge. I don't want to react, and I teach my kids not to react, but for others, it creates a thirst for revenge, and they don't care, even if they lose themselves."

That primal urge is understandable, as is the impulse to fight for freedom, independence and an end to Israel's 37-year occupation of Palestinian lands.

The continued genocide, of Israel's neighbors for 60 years now. Creating rebellion, and terrorist activity. Now aimed at the USA for the unwaivering support of such abuses.

WHAT SHOULD WE HAVE LEARNED LONG AGO?
Real democracy is based on respect for human dignity and self-determination and can only be accomplished by the will of the people, not by brute force.

Influential's to Israel projects encourage elected officials, policy makers, and public opinion leaders to visit sites in Israel in order to forge stronger bonds with Israel. These visits help forge an unforgettable bond with the State of Israel. (BUT) It set the stage for loosing the WAR in Iraq.

All Arab nations recognize the CONNECTION of the United States, AIPAC, and Israel. The blind support of the Middle East No. 1 enemy ISRAEL set the stage for a failure no matter how many troops you send to Iraq.

Yes, the Iraqi's wanted a Democracy free of Sadam, but not replaced with a government hand picked by the United States, Israel, and AIPAC for the interest of Israel and control of the resources by that coalition.

Until the issues with Israel are resolved FAIRLY there is no win, no win situation. 67 Resolutions against Israel, all attempts to control the aggression, and land grabs are vetoed by the USA. Israel has violated international laws, continues to do so and our officials will make no comment on the true causes of the problems in the Middle East. NOT ONE will meet the Press, or Face the nation with the absolute truth of policy and aid. No Middle East Country has been dealt with fairly by the USA. Israel interest first and foremost, and is the cause for complete failure. WHO is to blame, our complete administration, Senate, and Congress. All need to be replaced. There is no winning until we face the facts of the corruption & crimes of Israeli organized crime, and the connection with our officials..

The powers of: "Jewish supremacist". The oligarchs and the Zionists want total supremacy over our nation. Their puppet George Bush, just as in the Iraq war, is happy to serve these masters of the American political landscape. It is not just leaders of AIPAC that are being investigated for spying. George Bush has surrendered his presidency completely to this foreign power and shames every real American who has pride in our country.

The biggest roadblock to the "New World Order" and a sublimation of America and Europe to Jewish-supremacist globalize is Vladimir Putin .

The truth is that Putin in attempting to defend Russia from the power of the Jewish supremacists – is in effect, defending all Americans, and all people everywhere who cherish their freedom and heritage. He is Russian rather than American, but his heritage is far closer to the American people and our interests than the Jewish supremacist misanthropists.

The polls on supporting the atrocities of George Bush / Dick Cheney / Aipac & Israel's WAR , shows that only 28% of American people support any of the foreign or domestic policies of this administration.

80% of that 28% have less then a seventh grade education, listen to talk radio, don't comprehend if they can read & write, live in a double wide south of the Mason/Dixon line, and believes any thing a preacher tells them about RAPTURE, and the end of the world is coming.

The other 20% have a high school education in auto mechanics and wood shop, believe in prayer in school, even though they never pray except in fox holes or prison, but believe what propaganda they hear on Sunday mornings.

Thankfully 72% of Americans can read, write, and understand we need change from trusting the hypocrisy of Political & religious leaders of today, that are in reality embedded in CORRUPTION with organized crime. Bought by special interest and investments in Corporation greed.

2008 elections will prove interesting. Will the polls that show Americans concern actually bear it out? OR will the electronic voting machines be just another FIX and Fraud election. As in the Elections, of 2000 & 2004.

Florida in 2000---Ohio in 2004. Looks like they are setting up Missouri for 2008..

OXYMORON: BUSH REGIME---DEMOCRACY (2ND) LIBERATE--OCCUPY. (PRE-EMPTED)

OXYMORON: LIBERATE----OCCUPY

Liberate: To set free, as from oppression, confinement, or foreign control.

Occupy: To seize possession of and maintain control over by or as if by conquest.

Any person "world-wide" knows the difference, knows the lies from the beginning, except for the congress of the United States.

That alone is enough for Impeachment.

Barrack Obama & John Edwards are the only candidates willing to change it all for the interest of the American people, and Human rights around the world.

They will fight to stop all the atrocities and genocides presently going on in the Middle East, and around the World.

Pre-emptive plans to occupy are quite evident.

2nd Oxymoron: Bush / Cheney regime---
DEMOCRACY.

ONLY PATHWAY FOR CHANGE THE CONSTITUTION
IS IN JEOPARDY

THE BEST OPPORTUNITY AMERICANS HAVE:

READ AND PAY ATTENTION THE "GIG" IS UP!!

Former John F. Kennedy adviser and speechwriter Ted Sorensen says the similarities between JFK's candidacy in 1960 and Barack Obama's candidacy today are "striking."

Both Kennedy and Obama entered the race for the Democratic nomination as first-term U.S. senators in their 40s, and both were faced with obstacles many observers deemed insurmountable, Sorensen writes in an opinion piece in Britain's Guardian newspaper.

For Kennedy, the obstacles were his lack of experience when compared to other Democratic candidates and his Catholic heritage — no Catholic had ever been elected president up until that point.

Obama faces the same criticism for his lack of experience, and must overcome the reluctance of some to vote for a black presidential candidate.

The "subtly bigoted phrase" most often heard during Kennedy's campaign was that it was "too early" for a Catholic president, Sorensen recalls. "No doubt Obama will hear — or has already heard — similar sentiments about the color of his skin."

Kennedy and Obama were both Harvard-educated, and both entered the political limelight as the result of starring roles at the Democratic convention preceding their candidacies — Kennedy in 1956, when he nominated Adlai Stevenson, and Obama in 2004.

Both also gained national attention through their best-selling inspirational books. JFK's "Profiles in Courage" and Obama's "The Audacity of Hope."

"Both men immediately stood out as young, handsome, and eloquent new faces who attracted and excited ever larger and younger crowds at the grass-roots level," Sorensen writes.

"Both were cerebral rather than emotional speakers, relying on the communication of values and hope rather than cheap applause lines."

Sorensen concludes in the Guardian: "Above all, after eight years out of power and two bitter defeats, Democrats in 1960, like today, wanted a winner — and Kennedy, despite his supposed handicaps, was a winner."

Regarding civil rights, the Cuban missile crisis, the space race and moon landing, and other issues, Sorensen added, Kennedy "succeeded by demonstrating the same courage, imagination, compassion, judgment, and ability to lead and unite a troubled country that he had shown during his presidential campaign. I believe Obama will do the same."

To the American voters:

DEMOCRATS
INDEPENDANTS
GREEN PARTY
UNITY08
DIS-SATISFIED REPUBLICANS

BLACK, BROWN, YELLOW, WHITE, MALE , FEMALE, RELIGIOUS, OR NON- RELIGIOUS.

OUR CONSTITUTION HAS BEEN IN JEOPARDY FOR THE LAST 7 TO 15 YEARS.

We need to unite and defend our Country. It is our country, our Constitution, Not Mexico's, China's, India's, or Israel's. We can not continue under the present policies.

To insure that change will come about, we need to vote for the most promising candidates.

Senator Barrack Obama in all aspects should be our choice for 2008. Please listen to his message, and seriously follow his campaign. We the American people are "HIS SPECIAL INTEREST GROUP".

John Edwards should be our Vice President, One America for ALL AMERICANS. He stood up and said his vote on Iraq was wrong, he was the first to admit he was misled. HE was not forced into taken that position like many other polarized candidates, which follow special interest policies.

Congressman Dennis Kucinich has taken a position against War, has led toward Impeachment of the Crime Bosses now in office. He is a man of character & values that we need representing us with in our next administration.

Senator Biden has been a great leader, has proven knowledge in Foreign Affairs, and would protect our borders against "TERRORISM" with out attacking another Country. Would defend our Country, when and only when absolutely needed take proper military action. He would make the best Secretary of Defense, we could ever ask for.

There are candidates, that may make an announcement of running for office, but only after special interest groups commit tons of money to them, prior to announcing. Our answer, to them, stay home. We don't need you or want you.

All republican candidates should stay home with you; they all supported this past administration, even many Democrat candidates rubber stamped Bush. One candidate's husband traveled the World with Bush 1, all for Bush 2 and his policies. NOW they take a position against this administration. WHAT TO HELL kind of over-sight or accountability is that?

It certainly wasn't just Republicans that sat on their hands when it came to Katrina.

How many atrocities vs. the American people will it take to get Congress to impeach?

How the White House Drowned New Orleans.

We know now that Katrina's 1500 deaths didn't have to happen. The neglect of Bush based on his class/racial prejudice made him unconcerned to the pain and disaster then about to happen.

I believe the American people should support wholeheartedly the claim of our fellow Americans in New Orleans for reparations.

The whistleblower is Dr. Ivor van Heerden, deputy director of the Louisiana State University Hurricane Center, the chief technician advising the state on saving lives during Katrina. Understand that Katrina never hit New Orleans. The hurricane swung east of the city, so the state evacuation directors assumed New Orleans was now safe -- and evacuation could slow while emergency efforts moved east with the storm. But unknown to the state, in those crucial hours on Monday, the federal government's helicopters had filmed the cracks that would become walls of death by Tuesday.
"So the White House wouldn't tell you the levees had breeched?"
"They didn't tell anybody."
 Dr. Van Heerden: "I mean nobody knew. The Corps of Engineers knew. FEMA knew. None of us knew."

Under law dating back to 1935, a breech of the federal levee system makes the damage -- and the deaths -- a federal responsibility. Bush didn't take responsibility.

And what was the effect of the White House's self-serving delay? "Fifteen hundred people drowned. That's the bottom line."

They could have survived Hurricane Katrina. But they got no mercy from Hurricane George.

Barrack Obama and John Edwards stepped up immediately for our fellow Americans in New Orleans. All our minority Americans should step up and support who they knew fought for them, and continue to.

We all need to unite now, BASE your vote by your Heart and Mind, not the wallets of these special interest groups & propaganda paid for by them. Look at all the Atrocities, domestic and foreign.

For the benefit of Country people with unprecedented happenings. The above mentioned candidates know we need unprecedented leadership and unity. Step up and do what is best, and how you can best serve the Country, not yourself or the conglomerates presently in charge.

Barrack Obama's campaign is and has been supported by contributions of individual citizens, us the American people. Why, he brings his campaign to us, average America. NOT AIPAC or 60 other such organizations, or corporations.

That is the only pathway to change...........

WE CAN HAVE AN IMPEACHMENT BREAKOUT

The mainstream corporate media would like to pretend that there is nothing going on, but a 15th member of the House just signed on to Kucinich's H.Res. 333, Impeach Dick Cheney, first. 95,000 people have already voted in the National Cheney Impeachment Poll, and no matter how many times Pelosi protests that impeachment is off the table, we can drive it like a truck right through the front picture window. And this is how we are going to do it.

It is difficult to believe that with the U.S. establishment having all but conceded defeat in Iraq, and with the Baker-Hamilton Iraq Study Group having signaled that the United States needs the help of its rivals Iran and Syria – as well as Turkey, Saudi Arabia, and other influential Middle Eastern nations – to contain the Iraqi civil war, the U.S. and Israel are still pursuing the war and building permanent military bases in the disintegrating nation. Yet, this is precisely what the Pentagon is doing.

Whether the U.S. retains five or 15 "enduring bases," its goal is clear: to keep its military hand on the "jugular vein" of global capitalism – as former Joint Chiefs of Staff Chairman Maxwell Taylor described Middle East oil. This requires an intimidating infrastructure of deadly high-tech fortresses and the warriors that go with them.

All U.S. troops must be brought home if there is to be a chance for peace in Iraq. If the region's nations, are to have any hope of finally exercising self-determination. If the United States wants to regain the trust and support of the international community, its military bases must be closed – quickly and permanently.

It all depends on how submissive the rest of the WORLD is. Right now there is no notable objection.

Every Republican candidate for president is trying to distinguish himself from Bush, but the major candidates would carry forward Bush's core agenda:

President Giuliani would support a second escalation of the war in Iraq.1

President Romney would double the size of the Guantanamo Bay prison.2

President McCain would bomb, bomb, bomb Iran.3

President Fred Thompson would have offered Scooter Libby a full pardon.4

We can make sure the Bush era ends in 2008. But it means starting now, not next year: building strength in key neighborhoods, creating cutting-edge tools for volunteers, and designing the most sophisticated voter turnout effort progressives have ever run.

PAID BY ME: CITIZEN FOR CHANGE.

OBAMA--EDWARDS--KUCINICH--BIDEN

True patriots we need in the next administration to take our "Country Back"!!

CLINTON SPECIAL INTEREST, AIPAC, THE SAME LOBBY INFLUENCING BUSH & THE OTHER CRIME BOSSES:

IF AMERICA ELECTS CLINTON, IT WILL BE THE SAME BUSINESS AS USUAL. AIPAC, ISRAEL, & MOSSAD AT THE FOREFRONT.

AIPAC's hypocrisy is stomach-turning, to say the least. The goliath lobbying organization wants Iran to be slapped across the knuckles while the crimes of Israel continue to be ignored. And who is propping up AIPAC's hypocritical position? Senator, Hillary Clinton, of New York.

As Sen. Clinton embraces Israel's violence, as well as AIPAC's duplicitous Iran position, she simultaneously ignores the hostilities inflicted upon Palestine, as numerous Palestinians have been killed during the recent shelling of the Gaza Strip. Over the past weeks Israel continues to mark the occupied territories (they call 'buffer zones') like a frothing-mouth K9 on the loose.

Hillary Clinton's silence toward Israel's brutality implies the senator will continue to support AIPAC's mission to occupy the whole of the occupied territories, as well as a war on Iran in the future. AIPAC's right -- even President Bush appears to be a little sheepish when up against Hillary "warmonger" Clinton.

It is safe to say that Israel's bomb building techniques are light years ahead of Iran's dismal nuclear program.

AIPAC and Israel pressure the U.S. government to force the Iran issue to the U.N. Security Council, Israel itself stands in violation of numerous U.N. Resolutions dealing with the occupied territories of Palestine, including U.N. Resolution 1402, which demands that Israel withdraw its military from all Palestinian cities at once.

As the top Democratic recipient of pro-Israel funds for the 2006 election cycle thus far, pocketing over $58,000 as of October 31 last year, Senator Clinton now has Iran in her cross-hairs.

WE AMERICANS FEAR THIS USA GOVERNMENT AND ADMINISTRATION "MORE" THEN WE DO AL-QAEDA. (AN ORGANIZATION CREATED TO RESIST THE FOREIGN POLICIES BASED ON ISRAELI INTEREST, NOT AMERICA'S.)

.

We certainly know now that Republicans in power cannot be trusted with the Constitution or the Budget. OR ANYTHING FOR THAT MATTER:
Twice now they just found it easier to go off and make wars rather than tackle the real reforms America needs. Don't forget that Bush

Father also caved in on taxes & spending, once he started his war, just as his son followed the same path. The warfare state always pays homage to the Welfare State.
Freedom of expression consists of the rights to freedom of speech, press, assembly and to petition the government for a redress of grievances.

Many committees in the House and Senate, without taking any energy away from ending the war, can finally conduct the investigations that have gone undone for 6 years, exposing evidence that could very well lead to criminal, civil, or political accountability, as well as pressure to end the war and precedent to help prevent the next war.

American media. We have all seen what complacency in the media can bring. The Iraq War could not have been executed without it. Impeachment is being framed as a distraction or as revenge. It is time for the media to discuss the real evidence that supports Impeachment and leave the opining to the citizens of this country.

The case for impeachment is so strong that, recently, hardly a day goes by without more disclosures which strengthen any number of impeachable offenses that could form a Congressional action under our Constitution. An illegal war, to begin with, against our Constitution which says only Congress can declare war. An illegal war under domestic laws, and international law, and conducted illegally under international conventions to which the US belongs, should cause an outcry against this small clique of outlaws committing war crimes who have hijacked our national government.

By any legal standard and by the requirements of the U.S. Constitution (Article 1, Section 8, the war-declaring authority), George W. Bush and Dick Cheney are probably the most impeachable President and Vice President in American history.

What matters is that impeachment in this case - based on the authority of Congress to charge the President and Vice President with "high crimes and misdemeanors" - is a patriotic cause rooted in the wisdom of our founding fathers who did not want another King George III in the guise of a President.

Both George W. Bush and Dick Cheney should resign. They have disgraced their office and bled the nation. They have shattered the public trust in so many serious ways that will only become worse in the coming months. Not only America's trust: But the entire international community.

The "huge challenge" the Bush administration faces in trouble spots around the world. What takes place in Afghanistan, Egypt, Iran, Libya, Morocco, Pakistan, Saudi Arabia, Syria, Turkey and especially the Israeli-Palestinian relationship may well be as significant for the Middle East as what occurs in Iraq.

What happens in China, India, Russia, Europe and Africa may well be as important for the future of the international system as what transpires in the Middle East.

Diplomacy -- the oldest tool in international relations -- seems fated for revival. The people chosen to share leadership in the State Department and to represent the United States abroad must be skilled diplomats and not just Bush loyalists.

IT SEEMS obvious, doesn't it? If America cannot bring peace to Iraq, it should get out. Everyone now agrees that the old policy of "staying the course" will not work, so the debate in Washington today is between those who believe that some other strategy might work and should be tried, and those who think that nothing will, so America should get out now.

The White House delay prompted criticism from Democratic congressional leaders and from at least one Republican senator,

Chuck Hagel, who said President Bush was failing to show sufficient urgency about Iraq despite months of escalating violence.

BUSH: We will stay the course; we will complete the job in Iraq. BUSH: And so the United States of America will stay the course and we will complete the task. We'll help Iraq develop a democracy and the world will be better off for it. We're making steady progress. A free Iraq will mean a peaceful world. And it's very important for us to stay the course, and we will stay the course.

Nothing like this surprises us anymore. They know they can get away with this crap, so why not. It's all fun and games until 655,000 Iraqis are dead. Then its just fun... for Bush/Cheney, Israel, Mossad, and AIPAC, do they call it a "Justified Genocide".

Political scientists John Mearsheimer (U of Chicago) and Stephen Walt (Harvard) bravely take on the issue of the pro-Israel lobby in Washington and the way it distorts US foreign policy in the Middle East. Most American Jews deeply disagree with the policies advocated by the American Enterprise Institute, the Jewish Institute for National Security Affairs, etc., But a sliver of the political spectrum, falsely insisting that it represents all American Jews, manages to skew US politics and reporting on the issue of Palestine.

Anyone following the current situation in the Palestinian/Israeli relationship can clearly see that the Palestinians are boxed into a corner from which they cannot escape to construct a viable country.

With all the billions going to Israel for which no accounting is requested, then surely millions are cycled back to the US to corrupt Congress, look at the construction going on in Israel. Look close at the no bid contracts, and the Secret projects.

I wonder if anyone has been looking into the backwash of cash.

Jewish groups have launched petitions criticizing Carter's use of the word "apartheid" - the system of racial separation once used in South Africa - to describe Israel's treatment of the Palestinians.

Carter said that debate had been stifled by the media and others.

"It's almost a universal silence concerning anything that might be critical of current policies of the Israeli government," he said.

"Worse than apartheid"

Carter said he stands by his use of the "apartheid" and cited the fences, electric sensors and concrete slabs that Israel has built in the West Bank as an example of the divide.

The book follows the Israeli-Palestinian peace process, starting with Carter's 1977-1980 presidencies and the Camp David peace accord he negotiated between Israel and Egypt.

It blames Israel, the Palestinians, the US and many others, but it is most critical of Israel.

"Tremendous intimidation"

He added that the book had been vetted by Carter Centre staff and an unnamed "distinguished" reporter.

Carter, who won the Nobel Peace Prize in 2002, lamented the lack of discussion of Israeli policy in the US.

"There's a tremendous intimidation in this country that has silenced our people. And it's not just individuals; it's not just folks who are running for office. It's the news media as well," he said.

Carter, who has led efforts to monitor several elections in the Palestinian Territories since leaving office, said bringing peace to the Middle East is the most important commitment in his public life.

Real democracy is based on respect for human dignity and self-determination and can only be accomplished by the will of the people, not by brute force.

67 Resolutions against Israel, all attempts to control the aggression, and land grabs are vetoed by the USA. Israel has violated international laws, continues to do so and our officials will make no comment on the true causes of the problems in the Middle East. NOT ONE will meet the Press, or Face the nation with the absolute truth of policy and aid. No Middle East Country has been dealt with fairly by the USA. Israel interest first and foremost, and is the cause for complete failure. WHO is to blame, our complete administration, Senate, and Congress. All need to be replaced. There is no winning until we face the facts of the corruption & crimes of Israeli organized crime, and the connection with our officials..

The powers ofl "Jewish supremacist". The oligarchs and the Zionists want total supremacy over our nation. Their puppet George Bush, just as in the Iraq war, is happy to serve these masters of the American political landscape. It is not just leaders of AIPAC that are being investigated for spying. George Bush has surrendered his presidency completely to this foreign power and shames every real American who has pride in our country.
The biggest roadblock to the "New World Order" and a sublimation of America and Europe to Jewish-supremacist globalize is Vladimir Putin .

The truth is that Putin in attempting to defend Russia from the power of the Jewish supremacists – is in effect, defending all Americans, and all people everywhere who cherish their freedom and heritage. He is Russian rather than American, but his heritage is far closer to the American people and our interests than the Jewish supremacist misanthropists.

Many citizens concerned by the undue influence of the Israel lobby are dismayed by the action of the US Congress that adopts resolution after resolution favoring Israel with nary of word about its failure to make peace with the Palestinians, whose land it inhabits, or with its neighbors, whose borders it abutts. Last year Stephen Walt and John Mearsheimer, two professors from prestigious American universities, began a public debate on the power of the lobby - a cause long advocated by the Council for the National Interest - giving hope that a public airing of the American Israel Public Affairs Committee (AIPAC), its work, financing, and political connections would help Americans understand the gross misdirection of Middle East foreign policy over the last forty years. Grant F. Smith's new book, Foreign Agents, decisively pushes this debate forward and shows just how brazen and criminal the lobby has acted since its beginnings.

Smith traces the development of AIPAC from its early days under founder Si Kenen, who in 1947 registered with the US Department of Justice under the Foreign Agents Registration Act as an employee of the American Zionist Committee for Public Affairs. He was representing himself then as an agent working for Israel. He continued to register as a foreign agent during the late forties and fifties, working for various organizations funded by the Israel government, but in 1959, the name of the American Zionist Committee was changed to the American Israel Public Affairs Committee (AIPAC) to better reflect, as Kenen said, that it "raised its funds from both Zionists and non-Zionists." Its focus of work never changed, which was to promote the cause of Israel in both the executive and legislation branches of government, yet the organization no longer filed as a foreign agent. AIPAC eventually developed an extensive grassroots national network of organizations that engaged in all manner of illegal activities, from transgressing federal elections laws, to economic and industrial espionage, to flouting congressional laws regarding the use of arms exported to foreign countries, and passing classified and secret information to the Israeli government via the Israeli embassy in Washington. In 2005, after a nine-year investigation by the Federal Bureau of Investigation, two of AIPAC's top officials were arrested for espionage, and the role that AIPAC played over the years as a covert agent for Israel was given unusual light.

The book uses as a primary source the historic and remarkable hearings that Senator William Fulbright held in 1963 to investigate the "activities of agents of foreign principals in the United States." The Committee's aim was to look at the work of all organizations working on behalf of foreign countries, but in the process it discovered that the American Zionist Committee (AZC) was funded by the Jewish Agency, an arm of the Israeli government, and by the Israeli embassy, although its principals were not registered as foreign agents. The hearings disclosed the secret world of the AZC and the Jewish Agency, finding a pattern of money laundering that became a hallmark of AIPAC in the years to come. Both the Agency and the embassy typically hid the support that they provided by using private foundations and individuals as fronts so that it would appear the AZC was funded by American, not foreign, sources. Thus they bypassed the terms of the Foreign Agent Registration Act and sought to obscure their aim, which was to represent the interests of the Israeli government.

To measure the influence of the emerging lobby, Smith covers a wide spectrum of illegal and criminal activity. He begins by examining AIPAC's efforts to promote Israeli economic interests to the disadvantage of American workers. During the 1984 negotiations that preceded the creation of a "US-Israel Free Trade Agreement," AIPAC obtained a copy of the classified document spelling out the American negotiating strategy. Thus Israeli negotiators were aware of American positions well in advance of the meeting. AIPAC then managed to persuade the House Ways and Means Committee to provide special protections for Israeli imports of certain products should a free-trade zone be established. Even Congressional members, with long experience in Israeli lobby tactics, couldn't help but notice AIPAC's heavy hand in this instance.

The pressure exerted by AIPAC during congressional and presidential elections is well known, though consistently denied by the organization. Smith here focuses on the California Senate race of 1986 and the role played by Michael Goland, a real estate developer, who contributed $1 million via various conduits to derail a potential dangerous opponent of Sen. Alan Cranston, who was seeking reelection that year and was an AIPAC favorite. Goland was convicted and sentenced to imprisonment for election fraud. Goland had been a member of the board of AIPAC and had been highly visible in AIPAC's successful effort to unseat Sen. Charles Percy of Illinois in 1984.

AIPAC also had a hand in the defeat of Sen. Fulbright in 1968, and of Congressman Paul Findley in 1986. Findley's series of books about the lobby, especially his Dare to Speak Out, have been noted for the light they have thrown on the power of the lobby and its illegal activities.

AIPAC set up a series of political action committees (PACs), all with innocuous names, with the aim of influencing the election of congressional representatives all over the country. It made sure that internal firewalls, as Smith describes them, were set up so that no one could detect AIPAC's hand. But the line between them and the actions of the committees was hardly invisible. One "activist," a Chicago businessman, attempted to explain in a New York Times interview in 1987 how he and AIPAC operated independently, in the course of which it became apparent that the opposite was true, that there was tight coordination between AIPAC and dozens on pro-Israel committees. In 1988 the Washington Post published an internal AIPAC memo, reproduced in Foreign Agents, revealing now active AIPAC was in illegally coordinating PAC distributions to favored candidates.

The many instances of election fraud prompted a group of former US government officials to sue the Federal Election Commission for failure to require AIPAC to publish details of its income and expenditures, which political action committees are required to do. Among this group were George Ball, former secretary of state, Paul Findley, former congressman and founder of the Council for the National Interest, Andrew Kilgore, publisher of the Washington Report for Middle East Affairs and former ambassador to Qatar, and James Akin, former ambassador to Saudi Arabia. The FEC delivered a report on the complaint that cleared the PACs but professed a desire to further study the actions of AIPAC, but in fact the chief complaints were ignored. Appeals to the Supreme Court were turned aside on various points and the case remains in legal limbo to this day.

In the last twenty years, AIPAC has continued to develop its political networks. Steve Rosen, AIPAC Director of Policy, notoriously likened the lobby to "a night flower. It thrives in the dark and dies in the sun." It funds dozens of congressional "educational" trips to Israel every year through its affiliate the American Israel Education Foundation; it continues to publish Si Kenen's Near East Report, which serves as a propaganda arm of the Israel government; it established a "think tank," the Washington Institute for Near East Policy, which maintains a roster of "experts" providing cover for Israeli government positions (many of whose Board members have served as Board members of AIPAC); it maintains a large public relations office in Manhattan; and works in tandem with the new Saban Center for Middle East Policy, whose president, Martin Indyk, was deputy director of AIPAC and a former US ambassador to Israel. Thus Middle East policy at Brookings Institution, once a formidable independent think tank, has been usurped by pro-Israeli interests.

The growing arrogance of AIPAC, which in recent years acted with brazen impunity, was not unnoticed by the FBI counterintelligience which began probing the organization's activities as far back as 1999. In 2005, Col. Lawrence Franklin, who was working in the office of Douglas Feith, Undersecretary of Defense for Policy, was arrested and charged with giving classified documents to two top officials at AIPAC who passed them on to the Israeli embassy. The information concerned US positions toward Iran. The AIPAC officials were also arrested and charged with espionage. Lawrence was found guilty and sentenced to 12 years and seven months in prison and fined $10,000 for passing classified information to AIPAC and an Israeli diplomat. The trial against Steven Rosen and Keith Weissman has been delayed on several occasions and is now scheduled to begin in January 2008. The espionage charges have been dropped. A full analysis of the trial and its various permutations can be found in Smith's Chapter Five.

The case appropriately summarizes the extent of the illegalities that AIPAC has engaged in since its beginnings some fifty years ago. Senator Fulbright was on to something much bigger than even he could have imagined. Spawned by the Jewish Agency, it has abetted efforts that have encouraged "charitable" organizations in the US to contribute more than US $50 billion to illegal settlements in Gaza and the West Bank while appropriating and developing lands that belong to Palestinians. The money laundering activities of the Agency and the US donors have been brought to the attention of the US Department of Justice, thanks to work by the Institute for Research: Middle Eastern Policy and the Council for the National Interest but as yet no action has taken place to stop the illegal operations. As Smith states, "This follows an established pattern of law enforcement failures since the Fulbright foreign agent hearings."

Foreign Agents shines light on the murky world of AIPAC and its efforts to divert policy and push Israel's rightwing interventionist agenda in Washington. It garnered support for a war and occupation of Iraq in Congress. Contrary to the assertions of many now claiming how AIPAC was not promoting war, Smith documents how it helped prompt the American invasion of Iraq and now threatens to coordinate an intervention by the US in Iran. The consequences for the American public have been huge, as the response to Hurricane Katrina made clear, and has rendered the US the least popular country in the world. The book also discusses in detail how tenuous are AIPAC's claims to even be a legally constituted nonprofit corporation. Most of all, it serves to remind us that the American Israel Public Affairs Committee does not serve US interests, but works as a foreign agent for the government of Israel and should be required to register as a foreign agent. Only then will be operations and financing be made transparent and public. In fact, this book makes a convincing case that America - and the world - would be better off without AIPAC.

2008 elections will prove interesting. Will the polls that show Americans concern actually bear it out? OR will the electronic voting machines be just another FIX and Fraud election. Florida in 2000---Ohio in 2004. Looks like they are setting up Missouri for 2008..

Any person "world-wide" knows the difference, knows the lies from the beginning, except for the congress of the United States.

That alone is enough for Impeachment.

The "subtly bigoted phrase" most often heard during Kennedy's campaign was that it was "too early" for a Catholic president, Sorensen recalls. "No doubt Obama will hear — or has already heard — similar sentiments about the color of his skin."

Regarding civil rights, the Cuban missile crisis, the space race and moon landing, and other issues, Sorensen added, Kennedy "succeeded by demonstrating the same courage, imagination, compassion, judgment, and ability to lead and unite a troubled country that he had shown during his presidential campaign. I believe Obama will do the same."

To the American voters:

OUR CONSTITUTION HAS BEEN IN JEOPARDY
FOR THE LAST 7 TO 15 YEARS.

We need to unite and defend our Country.
It is our country, our Constitution, Not Mexico's, China's, India's, or Israel's. We can not continue under the present policies.

To insure that change will come about, we need to vote for the most promising candidates.

Senator Barrack Obama in all aspects should be our choice for 2008. Please listen to his message, and seriously follow his campaign. We the American people are "HIS SPECIAL INTEREST GROUP".

John Edwards should be our Vice President, One America for ALL AMERICANS. He stood up and said his vote on Iraq was wrong, he was the first to admit he was misled. HE was not forced into taken that position like many other polarized candidates, which follow special interest policies.

Congressman Dennis Kucinich has taken a position against War, has led toward Impeachment of the Crime Bosses now in office. He is a man of character & values that we need representing us with in our next administration.

Senator Biden has been a great leader, has proven knowledge in Foreign Affairs, and would protect our borders against "TERRORISM" with out attacking another Country it certainly wasn't just Republicans that sat on their hands when it came to Katrina.

Barrack Obama and John Edwards stepped up immediately for our fellow Americans in New Orleans. All our minority Americans should step up and support who they knew fought for them, and continue to.

We all need to unite now, BASE your vote by your Heart and Mind, not the wallets of these special interest groups & propaganda paid for by them. Look at all the Atrocities, domestic and foreign.

Barrack Obama's campaign is and has been supported by contributions of individual citizens, us the American people. Why, he brings his campaign to us, average America. NOT AIPAC or 60 other such organizations, or corporations.

It is difficult to believe that with the U.S. establishment having all but conceded defeat in Iraq, and with the Baker-Hamilton Iraq Study Group having signaled that the United States needs the help of its rivals Iran and Syria – as well as Turkey, Saudi Arabia, and other influential Middle Eastern nations – to contain the Iraqi civil war, the U.S. and Israel are still pursuing the war and building permanent military bases in the disintegrating nation. Yet, this is precisely what the Pentagon is doing.

Whether the U.S. retains five or 15 "enduring bases," its goal is clear: to keep its military hand on the "jugular vein" of global capitalism – as former Joint Chiefs of Staff Chairman Maxwell Taylor described Middle East oil. This requires an intimidating infrastructure of deadly high-tech fortresses and the warriors that go with them.

All U.S. troops must be brought home if there is to be a chance for peace in Iraq
It all depends on how submissive the rest of the WORLD is. Right now there is no notable objection.

Every Republican candidate for president is trying to distinguish himself from Bush, but the major candidates would carry forward Bush's core agenda:

President Giuliani would support a second escalation of the war in Iraq.1
President Romney would double the size of the Guantanamo Bay prison.2
President McCain would bomb, bomb, bomb Iran.3
President Fred Thompson would have offered Scooter Libby a full pardon.4
We can make sure the Bush era ends in 2008. But it means starting now, not next year: building strength in key neighborhoods, creating cutting-edge tools for volunteers, and designing the most sophisticated voter turnout effort progressives have ever run.

OBAMA--EDWARDS--KUCINICH--BIDEN
True patriots we need in the next administration to take our "Country Back".

As Sen. Clinton embraces Israel's violence, as well as AIPAC's duplicitous Iran position, she simultaneously ignores the hostilities inflicted upon Palestine, as numerous Palestinians have been killed during the recent shelling of the Gaza Strip. Over the past weeks Israel continues to mark the occupied territories (they call 'buffer zones') like a frothing-mouth K9 on the loose.

Hillary Clinton's silence toward Israel's brutality implies the senator will continue to support AIPAC's mission to occupy the whole of the occupied territories, as well as a war on Iran in the future. AIPAC's right -- even President Bush appears to be a little sheepish when up against Hillary "warmonger" Clinton.

It is safe to say that Israel's bomb building techniques are light years ahead of Iran's dismal nuclear program.

AIPAC and Israel pressure the U.S. government to force the Iran issue to the U.N. Security Council, Israel itself stands in violation of numerous U.N. Resolutions dealing with the occupied territories of Palestine, including U.N. Resolution 1402, which demands that Israel withdraw its military from all Palestinian cities at once.

As the top Democratic recipient of pro-Israel funds for the 2006 election cycle thus far, pocketing over $58,000 as of October 31 last year, Senator Clinton now has Iran in her cross-hairs.

Israel has most likely produced enough plutonium to make up to 200 nuclear weapons.

What matters is that impeachment in this case - based on the authority of Congress to charge the President and Vice President with "high crimes and misdemeanors" - is a patriotic cause rooted in the wisdom of our founding fathers who did not want another King George III in the guise of a President.

Both George W. Bush and Dick Cheney should resign. They have disgraced their office and bled the nation. They have shattered the public trust in so many serious ways that will only become worse in the coming months.
The "huge challenge" the Bush administration faces in trouble spots around the world. What takes place in Afghanistan, Egypt, Iran, Libya, Morocco, Pakistan, Saudi Arabia, Syria, Turkey and especially the Israeli-Palestinian relationship may well be as significant for the Middle East as what occurs in Iraq.

Diplomacy -- the oldest tool in international relations -- seems fated for revival. The people chosen to share leadership in the State Department and to represent the United States abroad must be skilled diplomats and not just Bush loyalists.

Everyone now agrees that the old policy of "staying the course" will not work, so the debate in Washington today is between those who believe that some other strategy might work and should be tried, and those who think that nothing will, so America should get out now.

The White House delay prompted criticism from Democratic congressional leaders and from at least one Republican senator, Chuck Hagel, who said President Bush was failing to show sufficient urgency about Iraq despite months of escalating violence.

Nothing like this surprises us anymore. They know they can get away with this crap, so why not. Its all fun and games until 655,000 Iraqis are dead. Then its just fun... for Bush/Cheney, Israel, Mossad, and AIPAC, do they call it a "Justified Genocide".

I think he deliberately lies just so he can get caught at it. That's one twisted individual.

Anyone following the current situation in the Palestinian/Israeli relationship can clearly see that the Palestinians are boxed into a corner from which they cannot escape to construct a viable country.

With all the billions going to Israel for which no accounting is requested, then surely millions are cycled back to the US to corrupt Congress, look at the construction going on in Israel. Look close at the no bid contracts, and the Secret projects.

I wonder if anyone has been looking into the backwash of cash.

Carter, who has led efforts to monitor several elections in the Palestinian Territories since leaving office, said bringing peace to the Middle East is the most important commitment in his public life.

All Arab nations recognize the CONNECTION of the United States, AIPAC, and Israel. The blind support of the Middle East No. 1 enemy ISRAEL set the stage for a failure no matter how many troops you send to Iraq.
Yes, the Iraqi's wanted a Democracy free of Sadam, but not replaced with a government hand picked by the United States, Israel, and AIPAC for the interest of Israel .
And control of the resources by that coalition. Until the issues with Israel are resolved FAIRLY there is no win, no win situation. 67 Resolutions against Israel, all attempts to control the aggression, and land grabs are vetoed by the USA. Israel has violated international laws, continues to do so and our officials will make no comment on the true causes of the problems in the Middle East.
NOT ONE will meet the Press, or Face the nation with the absolute truth of policy and aid. No Middle East Country has been dealt with fairly by the USA. Israel interest first and foremost, and is the cause for complete failure.
WHO is to blame, our complete administration, Senate, and Congress. All need to be replaced. There is no winning until we face the facts of the corruption & crimes of Israeli organized crime, and the connection with our officials..

Any one denying Israel's 58 years of terror in the Middle East, and the connection they continue to have in all Middle East problems have their heads in the sand, or are getting their pockets lined with the graft & corruption.

The Congress of the once United States of America has shown innumerable instances of being uncontrollable by the will of the people whom they represent.

Now we have to endure a willful Commander in Chief, a capitalistic Senate who will not leave a single penny to benefit the much needed education and infrastructure support of the States Governments.

History has shown that the American People cannot sustain any war and monetary drains caused by such wars. Neither can we sustain such trillions of United States Dollars going into underdeveloped countries which when they become developed by the influx of our dollars, then compete successfully against the very institutions who founded them. Does this sway our government? NO!

You're helping us build support for transformational change in early primary states and across the country.

Why is it that those who resist an illegal occupation of their land are considered freedom fighters except for those who resist an illegal Israeli occupation? In that case they are considered terrorists.

Why is it that when Israel abducts more than 9000 Palestinians this is called an arrest but when Hamas or Hezbollah abducts 2 Israeli soldiers it is called a kidnap?

Why is it when Hamas or Hezbollah fires a rocket into Israel it is considered an act of provocation but when Israel deliberately shells a Palestinian beach and kills 7 members of one family it is considered an act of self-defense?

Why does there exist such a double-standard? Why is that?

Why is it okay for the United States to supply Israel with cluster bombs and precision guided missiles and billions more of military weapons but wrong for Iran or Syria to supply Hezbollah with Kytusha rockets?

Why is it wrong for Iran to cultivate nuclear weapons when its neighbor, Israel, has hundreds of nuclear weapons aimed at it on land and on sea?

Why is it that UN Security Resolutions against Hezbollah must be complied with but those against Israel are ignored?

Why the double standard?

How long can we go on accepting this double standard?

If the United States wants to win this war on terrorism then getting tough with Israel would be the best step they could take. Politically, it is a hard choice, but ultimately a sensible and realistic one that would bring about true peace and justice in the Middle East.

ISRAEL DESERVES SERIOUS CONSEQUENCE

The special-interest industry in Washington has only grown since the last election, and it will spend more money than ever this time to try to own our political process and dictate our policies in Washington. Little federal aid for states White House, pushing tax cuts, says red ink may shrink state government the president made it clear last week that states will have to find their way out of their problems without much federal aid, as he pursues federal tax cuts that he said will stimulate economic growth.

"Listen, I'm sorry that states are in deficit, obviously," Bush said, in a transcript released by the National Journal. "Some states are raising taxes, some states are cutting expenditures. They are all meeting their deficits in different ways, but nevertheless, it is incumbent on the federal government to think in terms of how to enhance revenues."

Total federal aid to states and local governments in fiscal year 2004 was $408.1 billion

Now aid has been drastically reduced including
Health and Welfare to all States.

U.S. Financial Aid To Israel: Figures, Facts, and Impact
Total Cost to U.S. Taxpayers
$134,791,507,200

Total Taxpayer Cost per Israeli
$23,240

Total U.S. aid to Israel is approximately one-third of the American foreign-aid budget, even though Israel comprises just .001 percent of the world's population and already has one of the world's higher per capita incomes. No cuts have ever been discussed.

Israel ranks as the sixteenth wealthiest country in the world; Israelis enjoy a higher per capita income than oil-rich Saudi Arabia and are only slightly less well-off than most Western European countries.

Given Israel's relative prosperity, U.S. aid to Israel is becoming increasingly controversial. "Their economic situation is better than in many of our States, how can they go on asking for our charity?" Besides, asking our young people to die
for their benefit.

This means that U.S. government has given more federal aid to the average Israeli citizen in any given year than it has given to the average American citizen.

We are angry when we see Israeli settlers from Hebron destroy improvements made to Shuhada Street with our tax money. Also, it angers us that our government is giving over $10 billion to a country that is more prosperous than most of the other countries in the world and uses much of its money for strengthening its military and the oppression of the Palestinian people.
They have no respect for others in this world, never have had.

Most all U.S. aid to Israel took place after the June 1967 war, when Israel found itself more powerful than any combination of Arab armies...Yet it is our troops dying, not theirs from their cooked up intelligence.

The Aerospace Industry Association which promotes these massive arms shipments...is even more influential, or as influential as AIPAC. Then comes the investments into such by the Tax free Neo-cons, and their influence.Its force on Capitol Hill, in terms of lobbying, surpasses that of AIPAC at times.

The results," of the short-term thinking behind U.S. policy "are tragic," not just for the "immediate victims" but "eventually Israel itself" and "American interests in the region." The U.S. is sending enormous amounts of aid to the Middle East, and yet we are less secure than ever-both in terms of U.S. interests abroad and for individual Americans. Referring to the growing and increasing hostility the average Arab now has toward the United States. In the long term, peace and stability and cooperation with the vast Arab world is far more important for U.S. interests than this alliance with Israel.

This is not only an issue for those who are working for Palestinian rights, but it also jeopardizes the entire agenda of those of us concerned about human rights, concerned about arms control, concerned about international law.

The complete total of U.S. grants and loan guarantees to Israel for a fiscal year is $5,525,800,000. Sometimes plus.

Israel, whose troubles arise solely from its unwillingness to give back land it seized in the 1967 war in return for peace with its neighbors, does not fit any criteria for such aid.

The lobby that Israel and its supporters have built in the United States to make all this aid happen, and to ban discussion of it from the national dialogue, goes far beyond AIPAC, with its $15 million budget, its 150 employees, and its five or six registered lobbyists who manage to visit every member of Congress individually once or twice a year.

AIPAC, in turn, can draw upon the resources of the Conference of Presidents of Major American Jewish Organizations, a roof group set up solely to coordinate the efforts of some 52 national Jewish organizations on behalf of Israel.

ADL, it was shown, had added the illegally prepared and illegally obtained material to its own secret files, compiled by planting informants among Arab-American, African-American, anti-Apartheid and peace and justice groups.

The ADL infiltrators took notes of the names and remarks of speakers and members of audiences at programs organized by such groups. ADL agents even recorded the license plates of persons attending such programs and then suborned corrupt motor vehicles department employees or renegade police officers to identify the owners.

To date some 126 pro-Israel PACs have been registered, and no fewer than 50 have been active in every national election over the past generation.

There is something else very special about AIPAC's network of political action committees. Nearly all have deceptive names. Who could possibly know that the Delaware Valley Good Government Association in Philadelphia, San Franciscans for Good Government in California, Cactus PAC in Arizona, Beaver PAC in Wisconsin, and even Icepac in New York are really pro-Israel PACs under deep cover?

As a result, all but a handful of the 535 members of the Senate and House vote as AIPAC instruct when it comes to aid to Israel, or other aspects of U.S. Middle East policy. Will we attack Iran, certainly, if they give the order?

There is something else very special about AIPAC's network of political action committees. Nearly all have deceptive names. Who could possibly know that the Delaware Valley Good Government Association in Philadelphia, San Franciscans for Good Government in California, Cactus PAC in Arizona, Beaver PAC in Wisconsin, and even Icepac in New York are really pro-Israel PACs under deep cover?

According to the Population Reference Bureau of Washington, DC, the sub-Saharan countries have a combined population of 568 million. The foreign aid they have received by amounts to $42.99 per sub-Saharan African.

Similarly, with a combined population of 486 million, all of the countries of Latin America and the Caribbean together has received amounts to $79 per person.

A question that will never occur to the American public because, so long as America's mainstream media, Congress and president maintain their pact of silence, few Americans will ever know the true cost of Israel to U.S. taxpayers.

There are immense political and military costs to the U.S. for its consistent support of Israel during Israel's half-century of disputes with the Palestinians and all of its Arab neighbors.

Time to cut all Foreign Aid, until our own people are taken care of, and our deficits & Debts are paid.

DISABLIED VETERANS :(Is Our Military supported??)

The budget shortfalls have left the administrators shorthanded, but there's no excuse for not having checks for the disabled veterans, and we're going to get it corrected.
In some cases, while their claims work their way through the bureaucracy, the veterans are dying.
The Army denies intentionally pushing wounded soldiers off the military rolls.
The Army is systematically and deliberately underrating injured veterans' conditions to hold down costs
I hope America listened to Bob Woodruff.
Civilian casualties: claims 40,000 to maybe 100,000, when in fact it is known to be over 670,000 dead..

VA estimates that there are more than 250,000 homeless veterans in the Nation, or one-third of the adult homeless population.

Instead of providing adequate funds for the Department of Veterans Affairs (VA) medical system, the budget proposes to shift the cost burden onto the backs of veterans, making health care more expensive and even less accessible for millions of America's defenders.

As called for in the President's budget, total VA funding for the next fiscal year would increase about 1 percent, from the current $67.5 billion to $68.2 billion. More than half of the budget would go for mandatory programs such as disability compensation and pensions. Medical care for veterans would rise from $27.7 billion $27.8 billion with the bulk of that so-called increase coming almost entirely out of veterans' pockets.

The 1.2 million members disabled American Veterans across the country feel the inadequate appropriation.

Yet our foreign aid package to Israel: US congress has annually been approving a foreign aid bill totaling an average of $3 billion to Israel, $1.2 billion in economical aid, and $1.8 billion in military aid.

US has additionally been offering Israel $2 billion annually in federal loan guarantees, which brings the total US foreign aid to Israel to about $5 billion, or $13.7 million per day. This amount excludes the approximate $1.5 billion in total tax-deductible private donations from numerous Jewish charities and individual donors. All in all, this is the largest amount of foreign aid given to a country, and constitutes 30% of the total amount of US foreign aid budget.

For Peace in the Middle East,
Stop AIPAC!

The Annexation Wall surrounds the Palestinian village of Qalqilya. The wall deprives its 12,000 residents of their basic needs to work, to receive proper medical care, and to harvest their own land. AIPAC heavily lobbied Congress to support the Wall.

AIPAC had played a key role in fomenting support for the U.S. invasion of Iraq. It is playing an even greater role in supporting a future military strike against the people of Iran.

AIPAC, or the American Israel Public Affairs Committee, describes itself as the most important organization affecting the U.S. relationship with Israel. With a budget of $65 million, and membership now standing at over 100,000, it is no wonder that congressional staffers consider it one of the most powerful and effective lobbies on Capitol Hill.

Once a year, AIPAC holds its annual conference in Washington DC. This May it was attended by over 5,000 participants. Its annual policy conference is one of Washington's largest gatherings of lawmakers, topped only by the President's State of the Union address. Guests this year included two-thirds of the House, half the Senate, and Vice President Richard Cheney.

Only rarely is a critical word uttered among politicians regarding AIPAC and its associates that support unjust and aggressive (and disastrous) U.S. policies toward the peoples of the Middle East. We aim to change that.

For too long, policies that support Israeli militarism and occupation have gone unchallenged. Political voices raising even minor disagreements with prevailing policies are silenced or subject to campaigns of intimidation. We must open the door to full debate regarding U.S. relationship with Israel and U.S. policy with other countries in the region.

Demand a complete investigation of AIPAC, and that they be forced to register as a foreign agent, and pay taxes as they should. +++

The following statement is exactly what is wrong with our government today.

Where will your congressman, Senator, Governor, or any other representatives of America's government be.

I am out of the office from March 7 through March 13th at the AIPAC Policy Conference.

Then they will swear to you. That they work for Americans, not special interest, for foreign agency or representatives.

We want a list of all members that attend, so we will know who not to vote for in any and all future elections.

We no longer will put up with, foreign policy, speeches, bills written, by and for Israel, by AIPAC. We elected, pay and expect moral values, ethics, integrity, and honesty for America. We pay taxes for our interest not the evil regime.

That has been and is the major down fall of our government.

The pro-Israel lobby does most of its work without publicity. But every member of Congress and every would-be candidate for Congress comes to quickly understand a basic lesson. Money needed to run for office can come with great ease from supporters of Israel, provided that the candidate makes certain promises, in writing, to vote favorably on issues considered important to Israel. What drives much of congressional support for Israel is fear - fear that the pro-Israel lobby will either withhold campaign contributions or give money to one's opponent.

CHRISTIAN MORAL VALUES VS: RELIGIOUS ZIONIST HYPOCRISY GOOD VS: EVIL

Hypocrisy is the act of pretending or claiming to have beliefs, feelings, morals or virtues that one does not truly possess or practice. THE ZIONIST MOVEMENT.

CAN/WILL ANY REPUBLICAN EVER WIN AGAIN??

AIPAC, ISRAEL, & MOSSAD HAVE COMPLETELY DESTROYED THE REPUBLICAN PARTY, AND AMERICA'S STATUS IN THE WORLD!!

BE AMERICAN FIRST------FIGHT FOR AMERICA NOW:

The next few weeks are critical—Congress has the power to stop the war, but some representatives are afraid to use it. As Congress meets and debates, we need to remind them that bringing our troops home safely is what they were elected to do.

Voters elected Democrats in November to end the war. Now they have to step up and do it.

Friday, March 9, 2007
DoJ: FBI misused Patriot act in domestic spying activities:

As you've probably seen in today's headlines, the government is now reporting rampant FBI abuses of the Patriot Act's National Security Letter (NSL) provision that gives agents sweeping powers to demand sensitive personal records without court approval.
The report reveals that from 2003 to 2005, the government issued a staggering 143,000 National Security Letters, in some cases barring recipients from even reporting they've received a letter. How much more proof does Congress need that this dangerous provision defies democratic values? How many more of us will be investigated and gagged before the FBI is reined in?

There's only one course of action. It is time for Congress to repeal the expanded Patriot Act powers that opened the door to these abuses.

The FBI never needed and never should have been given these powers in the first place.

We'll keep fighting in the court of law and the court of public opinion until we take away these far-reaching powers that the Attorney General and the FBI shouldn't have and don't need.

Fight to restore the rule of law, and a government that's accountable to the Constitution.

For three years, the FBI understated to Congress how frequently it forced businesses to hand over that private information.

The FBI issued an estimated 47,000 letters in 2005.

A 2006 report to Congress shows that the FBI delivered only 9,254 national security letters during the 2005 year -

143,074 national security letters requesting customer data from businesses, the audit found. But that did not include an additional 8,850 requests that were never recorded in the FBI's database.

What this blunder of executive branch arrogance proves once again is clear - "trust us" is not how a well-functioning democracy operates.

NO ONE IN THE "WORLD" TRUSTS THIS GOVERNMENT. WHY TO HELL WOULD WE!!!

WHO IS ANTI-SEMITIC--WHO IS ANTI--AMERICAN

48% of the people of Jewish Faith residing in America, are opposed to the Lobby (AIPAC) and Other organizations. They do not believe that the actions of Israel are Justified. Nor do they want such government and organizations associated as Being a part of their faith. Are they really anti-Semitic as others are accused? Or are they proud to be American, and concerned About the direction of such foreign policy as lead by a lobby and its money trail.

They see this administration, the Zionist movement the same as we do. Anti-american.

Americans and Palestinians have in common Is the state of Israel legal?

What the American people and the Palestinian people have in common is both are victim of the Zionists. But the difference is although the Americans do not know this fact; the Palestinians know it very well. Americans do not fight it, because they are, among other things, very rich and have a bigger population to feel it. This fact affects the Palestinian considerably, because they do not have enough resources (human and economic). For example, if the Zionists in Israel kill three thousand of Palestinians who want to liberate their land (Palestine) that would affect the population considerably, but if they (Zionists) are the reason of killing three thousands American by sending them to, fight a war that they have nothing to do with them, Iraq the enemy of the state of Israel, three thousand of three hundred millions is just nothing. If the Zionists take away the tiny land of Palestine, that means that they took everything they owns, but if the Zionist take billions of dollars from us, they really did not take enough to divested us. The reason is because whatever the Zionists take away from America, it will still be minor. Taking away from huge America to give a tiny nation of Israel would not be noticeable, although, what the Zionists take away is too much compared to their population. If you do not know what the Zionist state take away for free from America, read James Petras' book "The Power of Israel in the United States". Nonetheless, it is a taboo; why American congress and each president of our country have to support the Zionists against the poor people of Palestine and allow these kinds of the give away of our human and economical resources without mentioning our political power of the Veto in the Security Council. If you look at the front and back cover and do not have to read Ilan Pappe's (Jewish historian) book "the Ethnic Cleansing of Palestine ", you will learn how we supported a crime against humanities.

The one billion dollar questions are: why did that fact happen? And how did we allow it to happen?

Although no one can give all the answers, there are some obvious reasons. The media, the press , and the campaign contributions. Our information system is controlled by the Zionists. The media and what comes with it from news to entertainments are controlled by Zionists. That the reason a lot of us do not know, not only, what the Zionists are doing in our country, but also, they do not know what the word "Zionists" means. Our education system is controlled by Zionists not only the books and curriculums, but also who is teaching them. The above components with other components conspire together to form a power that nobody knows where it came from and leave the people who are in public offices to afraid of opposing it and we become as bunch of zebras running away from the lion, because we are strong enough, but we can not coordinate our efforts to fight Zionism.

Conspiracy was not played only in America, but also played internationally. I believe that the whole world came together in around1948 and voted to allow the establishment of the state of Israel on the Palestinian land and the whole world gave a blind eye to the ethnic cleansing. How did these things happen? Before answering this question I would like to show what is happening in our State Department. If you do not know the name of the past American ambassadors to the UN. I will give you some names: Jeane Kirkpatrick, Richard Holbrooke, Nigrobonte, Albright, and so on, you will find them Zionists or pro-Zionists. You may probably heard about Andrew Young how was pressured to resigned the post of the UN ambassador because he denounced Israel for having "become the oppressor" of the Palestinians, for engaging in "terrorist" raids and "constant bombing" in Lebanon, and for "losing their moral advantage." Even John Bolton who supported the state of Israel has to leave the post because he said; "that settlement expansion must stop" and also its concern regarding "the route of the barrier" that Israel is constructing between the two states. So you can say there is a mechanism by which the Zionists can impose on America who can be and who can not be the ambassador of the US to the UN. If they can impose it on American they can impose it on the rest of the world. I believe they can impose it, also, on Moslem and Arab countries. I believe that the Zionists by 948 have enough Zionists or pro-Zionists to vote in the UN to allow them to move to Palestine. As this is just a belief and not confirmed, I ask you to ask your congress to make an investigation regarding: Firstly, if the whole world voting for the establishment of the state of Israel is legal. In other words, is the state of Israel legal? Secondly, why congress and all the presidents of the US support the Zionists and allow the them to get what no other race can get.

officials.

"WAR" who are we at war with :

Al-Qaida, not a Country, not a government, it is a terrorist organization. An organization that existed in Afghanistan. Had training camps and head quartered in Afghanistan.

Now, due to the actions of this administration, Israel and AIPAC lobby, we are in a Quagmire in Iraq. Why? Greed, their oil and a desire to Control the Middle East threw Israel.

Look at Palestine, Lebanon, Egypt, Jordan, Iran, Syria, Lybia, Kuwait, and Saudi Arabia. (The people of those countries) Those government leaders are all close to Losing control, of their people. The people now realize that the purpose of USA invasion was for occupation, permanent military bases and largest embassy in the world. NOT to liberate the people and leave on request as told by Bush in the beginning. To them and the American people.

The people associate the OCCUPATION, with the occupation by Israel of Palestinian lands. The people agree that Palestine has a right of return, but now see more and more people in refugee camps, with very sub-standard conditions, with No hope for assistance.

Al-qaida located in many countries now, Islam taking the blame for all the so called radicals & terrorist. HAS grown because those so oppressed have no where else to turn to rebel against the atrocities. Close to 1,000,000 innocent civilians killed. Millions forced to relocate.

The American people, know we were lied to, that our government is not representative of the America we once were. Now and for the last Six years we have asked for home security or border control. Realizing that terrorist organizations Exist all over the World, even on the home land, And can when they desire to, attack us from many Different directions.

An Indian walks into a cafe with a shotgun in one hand pulling a male buffalo with the other. He says to the waiter: "Want coffee." The waiter says, "Sure, Chief. Coming right up." He gets the Indian a tall mug of coffee. The Indian drinks the coffee down in one gulp, turns and blasts the buffalo with the shotgun, causing parts of the animal to splatter everywhere and then just walks out. The next morning the Indian returns. He has his shotgun in one hand, pulling another male buffalo with the other. He walks up to the counter and says to the waiter "Want coffee."

The waiter says "Whoa, Tonto! We're still cleaning up your mess from yesterday. What was all that about, anyway?" The Indian smiles and proudly says ."Training for position in United States Congress: Come in, drink coffee, shoot the bull, leave mess for others to clean up, disappear for rest of day.

Meanwhile:

The suicide rate in the US military is at a 30-year-high as American soldiers return from the Iraq war.

Homelessness among the Iraq veterans is also on the rise and Haggis says the US government is turning a blind eye to veterans' problems. He says 30,000 US soldiers have been told "you don't have post-traumatic stress syndrome, you have a pre-existing behavioural problem". They are not getting help from the government.

How many troops have died, how many injuried. 700,000 civilians killed.

I guess if you are dead, you are liberated.

What few Americans understand however, is the steep price they pay in many other fields for the U.S.-Israeli relationship, which in turn is a product of the influence of Israel's powerful U.S. lobby on American domestic politics and has nothing to do with U.S. strategic interests, U.S. national interests, or even with traditional American support for self-determination, human rights, and fair play overseas.

Besides its financial cost, unwavering U.S. support for Israel, whether it's right or wrong, exacts a huge price in American prestige and credibility overseas. Further, Israel's powerful U.S. lobby has been a major factor in delaying campaign finance reform, and also in the removal from American political life of some of our most distinguished public servants, members of Congress and even presidents.

Finally, the Israel-U.S. relationship has cost a significant number of American lives. The incidents in which hundreds of U.S. service personnel, diplomats, and civilians have been killed in the Middle East have been reported in the media. But the media seldom revisits these events, and scrupulously avoids analyzing why they occurred or compiling the cumulative toll of American deaths resulting from our Israel-centered Middle East policies.

Each of these four categories of the costs of Israel to the American people merits a talk of its own. What follows, therefore, is just an overview of such losses.

First is the financial cost of Israel to U.S. taxpayers. Between 1949 and 1998, the U.S. gave to Israel, with a self-declared population of 5.8 million people, more foreign aid than it gave to all of the countries of sub-Saharan Africa, all of the countries of Latin America, and all of the countries of the Caribbean combined – with a total population of 1,054,000,000 people.

In the 1997 fiscal year, for example, Israel received $3 billion from the foreign aid budget, at least $525 million from other U.S. budgets, and $2 billion in federal loan guarantees. So the 1997 total of U.S. grants and loan guarantees to Israel was $5.5 billion. That's $15,068,493 per day, 365 days a year.

If you add its foreign aid grants and loans, plus the approximate totals of grants to Israel from other parts of the U.S. federal budget, Israel has received since 1949 a grand total of $84.8 billion, excluding the $10 billion in U.S. government loan guarantees it has drawn to date.

And if you calculate what the U.S. has had to pay in interest to borrow this money to give to Israel, the cost of Israel to U.S. taxpayers rises to $134.8 billion, not adjusted for inflation.

Put another way, the nearly $14,630 every one of 5.8 million Israelis had received from the U.S. government by October 31, 1997, cost American taxpayers $23,241 per Israeli. That's $116,205 for every Israeli family of five.

None of these figures include the private donations by Americans to Israeli charities, which initially constituted about one quarter of Israel's budget, and today approach $1 billion annually. In addition to the negative effect of these donations on the U.S. balance of payments, the donors also deduct them from their U.S. income taxes, creating another large drain on the U.S. treasury.

Nor do the figures above include any of the indirect financial costs of Israel to the United States, which cannot be tallied. One example is the cost to U.S. manufacturers of the Arab boycott, surely in the billions of dollars by now. Another example is the cost to U.S. consumers of the price of petroleum, which surged to such heights that it set off a world-wide recession during the Arab oil boycott imposed in reaction to U.S. support of Israel in the 1973 war.

Other examples are a portion of the costs of maintaining large U.S. Sixth Fleet naval forces in the Mediterranean, primarily to protect Israel, and military air units at the Aviano base in Italy, not to mention the staggering costs of frequent deployments to the Arabian Peninsula and Gulf area of land and air forces from the United States and naval units from the Seventh Fleet, which normally operates in the Pacific Ocean.

Many years ago the late Undersecretary of State George Ball estimated the true financial cost of Israel to the United States at $11 billion a year. Since then direct U.S. foreign aid to Israel has nearly doubled, and simply adjusting that original figure into 1998 dollars would send it considerably higher today.

Next comes the cost of Israel to the international prestige and credibility of the United States. Americans seem constantly astounded at our foreign policy failures in the Middle East. This stems from a profound ignorance of the background of the Israeli-Palestinian dispute, which in turn results from a reluctance by the mainstream U.S. media to present these facts objectively.

Toward the end of the 19th century when political Zionism was created in Europe, Jews were a tiny fraction of the population of the Holy Land, much of which was heavily cultivated and thickly populated, and certainly not a desert waiting to be reclaimed by outsiders.

Even in 1947, after half a century of Zionist immigration and an influx of Jewish refugees from Hitler, Jews still constituted only one third of the population of the British Mandate of Palestine. Only seven percent of the land was Jewish-owned. Yet when the United Nations partitioned Palestine in that year, the Jewish state-to-be received 53 percent and the Arab state-to-be received only 47 percent of the land. Jerusalem was to remain separate under international supervision, a "corpus seperatum" in the words of the United Nations.

One of the myths that many Americans still believe is that the initial war between the Arabs and Israelis broke out on May 15, 1948 when the British withdrew and military units from Egypt, Jordan, Iraq and Syria entered Palestine, allegedly because the Arabs had rejected a partition plan that the Israelis accepted.

In fact, the fighting began almost six months earlier, immediately after the partition plan was announced. By the time the Arab armies intervened in May, some 400,000 Palestinians already had fled or been driven from their homes. To the Arab nations the military forces they sent to Palestine were on a rescue mission to halt the dispossession of Palestinians from the areas the U.N. had awarded to both the Jewish and the Palestinian Arab state. In fact history has revealed that the Jordanian forces had orders not to venture into areas the U.N. had awarded to Israel.

Although the newly created Israeli government didn't formally reject the partition plan, in practice it never accepted the plan. To this day, half a century later, Israel still refuses to define its borders.

In fact, when the fighting of 1947 and 1948 ended, the State of Israel occupied half of Jerusalem and 78 percent of the former mandate of Palestine. About 750,000 Muslim and Christian Palestinians had been driven from towns, villages and homes to which the Israeli forces never allowed them to return.

The four wars that followed, three of them started by Israel in 1956, 1967, and 1982, and one of them started by Egypt and Syria to recover their occupied lands in 1973, have been over the portions of Lebanon, Syria, Jordan and Egypt which the Israelis occupied militarily in those wars, the other half of Jerusalem, and the 22 percent of Palestine – comprising the West Bank and Gaza – which is all that remains for the Palestinians.

It is the unwillingness of successive U.S. governments to acknowledge these historical facts, and adjust U.S. Middle East policies to right these wrongs, that has resulted in such a devastating loss of international credibility. Americans, who once were identified with the modern schools, universities and hospitals they had established throughout the Middle East starting more than 150 years ago, now are identified with U.S. misuse of its veto in the United Nations to condone Israeli violations of the human rights of the Palestinians living in the lands Israel has seized by force. The Israeli occupation violates the preface to the United Nations Charter banning the acquisition of territory by war. What the Israeli government has been doing in the occupied territories also violates the Fourth Geneva convention, which forbids the transfer of populations to or from such areas.

Governments of Middle Eastern countries which once looked to the United States as their protectors from European colonialism, now find it very difficult to justify maintaining cordial relations with the United States at all. Friendly Arab governments are jeopardized by their U.S. alliances, and the fall of one, the Hashemite Kingdom of Iraq, was directly attributable to its premature withdrawal of its armed forces from Palestine during the 1948 fighting, and its subsequent membership in a military alliance with the U.S. and Britain.

Even our European and Asian allies have joined in deploring the perpetual American tilt toward Israel. In a recent vote on a U.N. General Assembly resolution calling upon Israel to curb further encroachments on Palestinian lands by Jewish settlers, only the United States and Micronesia voted with Israel. Of the 185 U.N. member nations, all of the others, without exception, voted against Israel or abstained.

Yet Americans seem oblivious to such examples of how their Israel-centered Middle East policies are isolating the United States in the world.

Next is the cost of Israel to the American domestic political system. In December 1997, Fortune magazine asked professional lobbyists to select the most powerful special interest group in the United States. They chose the American Association of Retired Persons, which lobbies on behalf of all Americans over 60.

In second place, however, was the American Israel Public Affairs Committee, Israel's official Washington, D.C. lobby, with a $15 million budget – the sources of which AIPAC refuses to disclose – and 150 employees. AIPAC, in turn, can draw upon the resources of the Conference of Presidents of Major American Jewish Organizations, a roof group set up to coordinate the efforts on behalf of Israel of some 52 national Jewish organizations.

Among those organizations are groups such as B'nai B'rith's Anti-Defamation League (ADL), with a $45 million budget, and

Hadassah, the Zionist women's group, which spends more than AIPAC and sends thousands of Americans every year to Israel on Israeli government-supervised visits.

Both AIPAC and the ADL maintain secret "opposition research" departments which compile files on politicians, journalists, academics and organizations, and circulate this information through local Jewish community councils to pro-Israel groups and activists in order to damage the reputations of those who dare to speak out and thus have been blackballed as "enemies of Israel." In the case of ADL, police raids on the organization's Los Angeles and San Francisco offices established that much of the information they had compiled was erroneous, and thus slanderous, and some also was illegally obtained.

In the case of AIPAC, this is not the organization's most controversial activity. In the 1970s members of AIPAC's national board of directors set out to form deceptively named local political action committees (PACs) which could coordinate their efforts in supporting candidates in federal elections. To date, at least 126 pro-Israel PACs have been registered, and no fewer than 50 PACs, like AIPAC, can give a candidate who is facing a tough opponent and who has voted according to AIPAC recommendations up to half a million dollars. That's enough money to buy all the television time needed to get elected in most parts of the country.

What is totally unique about AIPAC's network of political action committees is that they all have deceptive names. Who could possibly know that the Delaware Valley PAC in Philadelphia, San Franciscans for Good Government in California, Cactus PAC in Arizona, Chili PAC in New Mexico, Beaver PAC in Wisconsin and even Ice PAC in New York are really pro-Israel PACs. So just as no other special interest can put so much hard money into any candidate's election campaign as can the Israel lobby, no other special interest has gone to such elaborate lengths to hide its tracks.

Some of America's wisest and most distinguished public servants have been kept from higher office by the blackballing of the Israel lobby. One such leader was George Ball, who served the Kennedy administration as Under Secretary of State and the Johnson administration as U.S. Ambassador to the United Nations. Given his unmatched brilliance in forecasting international developments, there is no doubt that he would have become secretary of state had he not publicly expressed the skepticism about the U.S. relationship with Israel which most Americans involved in foreign affairs privately feel.

In membership meetings which journalists are not allowed to attend, AIPAC presidents have boasted that the organization was responsible for the defeats of two of history's most distinguished chairmen of the Senate Foreign Relations Committee – Democrat J. William Fulbright of Arkansas and Republican Charles Percy of Illinois. The list of other senators and House members for whose election defeats AIPAC takes credit is too long to recount.

There is good evidence also that had it not been for complex maneuvers by the Israel lobby, including encouragement of third party candidates and unrelenting partisanship by pro-Israeli syndicated columnists and other media figures, Democratic President Jimmy Carter probably would have been reelected in 1980, and Republican President George Bush almost certainly would have been reelected in 1992.

The cost to our political system of losing national figures who refused to allow U.S. domestic political interests to dictate U.S. foreign policy has been enormous. So long as AIPAC and other powerful lobbies continue to thwart meaningful efforts on behalf of campaign finance reform, Americans will continue unknowingly paying such costs.

Finally, there is the cost of Israel in American lives. References to the attack by Israeli aircraft and torpedo boats on the USS Liberty in which 34 Americans were killed and 171 wounded on the fourth day of the Six-Day War of June 1967 often are met by disbelief. Very few

Americans seem to have heard of the attack on the ship operated by the U.S. Navy for the National Security Agency to monitor Israel and Arab military communications during the fighting.

The Israeli government claimed it was a case of mistaken identity. The members of the crew and other naval officers who were stationed in the Mediterranean and in Washington at the time state that it was a deliberate attempt to sink the ship and blame Egyptian forces for the disaster. It is the only such event in U.S. Naval history the cause of which has never been formally investigated either by Congress or by the Navy itself.

Major losses of American lives at the hands of Arab forces opposing Israel are better known. These include the loss of 141 U.S. service personnel in the bombing of the U.S. Marine barracks in Beirut in 1984. They also include the loss of xx U.S. diplomats and xxx local employees of the U.S. government in two bombings of the American Embassy in Beirut. Other such events include the bombing of the U.S. Embassy in Kuwait, the taking of U.S. hostages in Beirut of whom three were killed, the deaths of Americans in a series of Middle East related skyjackings, the deaths of 19 U.S. service personnel in the bombing of the Al Khobar Towers in Saudi Arabia, and the 1997 assassination of four U.S. accountants working for an American company in Karachi.

All of these incidents, and many more in which Americans have died, resulted directly from one-sided U.S. support for Israel in its refusal to participate in the land-for-peace settlement with the Palestinians and its other Arab neighbors envisioned in U.N. Security Council Resolution 242. The U.S. has given lip service to that resolution since November, 1967. But in practice the U.S. has done nothing to force Israel to comply, even though the resolution has been accepted by the members of the League of Arab States. That U.S. hypocrisy fuels rage and frustration throughout the Middle East and South Asia which will continue to take a toll of American lives until Israel finally gives back the lands it occupied in 1967, or the U.S. stops subsidizing Israeli intransigence.

Claims that there are positive aspects of the U.S.-Israeli relationship seldom stand up to scrutiny. During the Reagan administration it was labeled for the first time a "strategic relationship" conferring benefits on the U.S. as well as on Israel. The idea that Israel – smaller in both area and population than Hong Kong – can offer the United States benefits sufficient to offset the hostility that relationship arouses among 250 million Arabs living in a 4,000-mile strategic swath of territory stretching from Morocco to Oman is ludicrous. It becomes even more ludicrous when one realizes that the relationship also has alienated another 750 million Muslims who, together with the Arabs, control more than 60 percent of the world's proven oil and gas reserves.

Apologists for Israel also describe the U.S.-Israeli cooperation in weapons development. The fact is that the one or two successful joint weapons programs have been largely U.S. financed, while for their part the Israelis have repeatedly sold to rogue nations U.S. weapons turned over at no cost to Israel.

It is a sad but proven fact that the Israeli government also has obtained secret U.S. military technology which Israel has sold to other countries. For example, after the U.S. sent Patriot missile defense batteries on an emergency basis to help defend Israel during the Gulf War, the Israelis seem to have sold the Patriot missile technology to China, according to the U.S. State Department's inspector general. As a result, the U.S. has been forced to develop a whole new generation of missile technology able to penetrate the defenses China has developed as a result of the Israeli treachery.

Perhaps the most hypocritical rationalization offered by friends of Israel is that U.S. special treatment is justified because Israel is "the Middle East's only working democracy" and that Israel and the U.S. have many basic institutions in common. In fact, Israeli democracy does not work for non-Jews. In contrast to the United States, where by law all citizens have equal rights regardless of religion or ethnic origin, Muslim and Christian citizens of Israel do not have equal rights with regards to military service, the extensive social benefits available to veterans of Israeli military service, or even in terms of Israeli tax rates imposed on Arab citizens and Israeli government expenditures in Arab communities within Israel.

Further, Israeli citizenship is not available to the Muslim and Christian Palestinians driven from their homes in Israel in 1948, nor to their descendants. But a Jew, born anywhere in the world, can have Israeli citizenship for the asking.

Perhaps most shocking is the little-known fact that by now 90 percent of the land in Israel proper is held under restrictive covenants barring non-Jews, even those with Israeli citizenship, from owning the land or from earning a living on it. Unfortunately, the land held under such covenants is increasing, not decreasing. It would be difficult, therefore, to find two countries more profoundly different in their approaches to basic questions of citizenship and civil and human rights as are the United States and Israel.

Watch the movie: "Valley of Elah"

This government now faces revolution from the
American people, there has never been a time
That the American people were so angry due to
None of the official representatives actually
Represent the PEOPLE, they are there bought
And paid for by special interest, represent
Corruption, foreign lobbies, organized crime,
 huge corporations foreign & domestic.

The Elites wanting GLOBALIZATION, which will
Never happen. NONE of the PEOPLE of any
Country will allow such. COMPLETE rebellion around
 the World is on the verge of happening.

WE SUPPORT OUR TROOPS,
BRING THEM HOME !!

The Executive Order entitled "Blocking Property of Certain Persons Who Threaten Stabilization Efforts in Iraq" provides the President with the authority to confiscate the assets of whoever opposes the US led war.

A presidential Executive Order issued on July 17th, repeals with the stroke of a pen the right to dissent and to oppose the Pentagon's military agenda in Iraq.

During the past two-weeks you have stepped up as never before and helped us demonstrate to our leaders in Congress that there will be a political price to pay if they refuse to defend our Constitutional freedoms.

In fact, you've stepped up in such a huge way we've decided to expand our efforts with an online version of our "Congress as Sheep" ads which will begin running today.

Remember, this is only the beginning of our campaign to demand that Congress act immediately to restore the Constitution. We intend to create a groundswell that will force a timid Congress to clean up the mess it made when it gave Bush sweeping new powers to spy on Americans and by demanding that Members of Congress act now to disavow torture, restore habeas corpus, and shut down Guantánamo prison.

Your support is more important than ever, as the Bush administration is already busy laying the groundwork for even more changes to FISA when Congress returns in the fall.

Director of National Intelligence Mike McConnell -- who played a large role in lobbying members of Congress to pass the recent FISA legislation -- has recently started stirring the pot anew. And he has repeatedly implied that those who insist on a full debate of these issues or who fail to bend to the Administration's demands are putting American lives at risk.

Continuing an appalling pattern under which government officials strategically and selectively disclose classified information in order to advance the administration's legislative agenda, Director McConnell made politically motivated comments that included references to previously classified court rulings from the Foreign Intelligence Surveillance Court (FISC). These are the same court orders that we have asked the FISC to disclose to the public.

This may be one of the most important efforts you or I will ever be involved in. Let's not let off the pressure for even one second.

The U.S. government is on a 'burning platform' of unsustainable policies and practices with fiscal deficits, chronic healthcare under funding, immigration, and overseas military commitments threatening a crisis if action is not taken soon, the country's top government inspector has warned.

David Walker, comptroller general of the U.S., issued the unusually downbeat assessment of his country's future in a report that lays out what he called "chilling long-term simulations."

These include "dramatic" tax rises, slashed government services, and the large-scale dumping by foreign governments of holdings of U.S. debt.

Drawing parallels with the end of the Roman Empire, there are "striking similarities" between America's current situation and the factors that brought down Rome, including "declining moral values and political civility at home, an over-confident and over-extended military in foreign lands, and fiscal irresponsibility by the central government."

"One of the concerns is obviously we are a great country but we face major sustainability challenges that we are not taking seriously enough, the fiscal imbalance means the U.S. is "on a path toward an explosion of debt."

With the looming retirement of baby boomers, spiraling healthcare costs, plummeting savings rates, and increasing reliance on foreign lenders, we face unprecedented fiscal risks.

Our very prosperity is placing greater demands on our physical infrastructure. Billions of dollars will be needed to modernize everything from highways and airports to water and sewage systems. America's fiscal, healthcare, education, energy, environment, immigration, and Iraq policies are in need of review and revision. Timely action is needed because Washington's historical crisis-management approach to dealing with hard public policy choices is no longer prudent.

The U.S. has faced big challenges in the past and it has always risen to them. However, we must not take comfort in our nation's current superpower status and past success. For a lesson in what we should avoid, we must learn from history. In this regard, the Roman Republic fell for a number of reasons and three in particular resonate today.

While it is unlikely that any reforms will occur during the balance of the Bush administration, some meaningful progress should be made before January 2009. Elected officials need to work to pass tough budget controls to help slow our fiscal hemorrhaging. They must also work with an Accountability Office to enhance transparency, targeting current financial reporting practices and budgeting processes. Last, create a capable, credible, and ethical commission to set the stage for significant reforms in 2009. That most likely is the one thing to be outsourced.

At present we no longer can find that kind of official in America.

Who is accountable for Rubber Stamping the President's disastrous policies for America?

Not only republicans give him the green light.

The special-interest industry in Washington has only grown since the last election, and it will spend more money than ever this time to continue to own our political process and dictate our policies in Washington.

We need a a stronger lobby reform bill to change the way Washington does business, all sides of The isle. Campaign & ear-mark reform.

Iraq war will cost America One Trillion dollars plus.
Life, limb, property, and our democracy.

The national Debt is at eight and three quarters, of a trillion dollars. If unfunded future obligations are added (i.e. Medicare and Social Security) this figure rises dramatically to a total of $59.1 Trillion

The trade deficit: The US has been borrowing from willing foreigners to maintain its lifestyle, even as we have become uncompetitive in world manufacturing markets.

The US is importing $850 Billion more in goods and services than it sells abroad.

The Trade Deficit is at unsustainable levels.

It is a malignant tumor in the intestines of the U.S. economy.

Wages in America were at an average of $15.91 per hour, NOW due to influx of illegal immigrants, and out sourcing of jobs The average dropped to $13.25. With lower Wage jobs the only ones on the rise. While prices and corporate profits are at all time highs. Rich get Richer, poor get poorer, and the middle class disappears.

Foreign aid package to Israel: US congress has annually been approving a foreign aid bill totaling an average of $3 billion to Israel, $1.2 billion in economical aid, and $1.8 billion in military aid.

US has additionally been offering Israel $2 billion annually in federal loan guarantees, which brings the total US foreign aid to Israel to about $5 billion, or $13.7 million per day. This amount excludes the approximate $1.5 billion in total tax-deductible private donations from numerous Jewish charities and individual donors. All in all, this is the largest amount of foreign aid given to a country, and constitutes 30% + of the total amount of US foreign aid budget. Why?? AIPAC purchase of congress..

"To announce that there must be no criticism of the president, or that we are to stand by the president right or wrong, is not only unpatriotic and servile, but is morally "Treasonable" to the American Public!!

HOW TO LIBERATE----BOMB THEM TO KINGDOM COME !!

Persistent aggressions by the Zionists are making life more and more difficult for the rightful owners of the land of Palestine. In broad day-light, in front of cameras and before the eyes of the world, they are bombarding innocent defenseless civilians, bulldozing houses, firing machine guns at students in the streets and alleys, and subjecting their families to endless grief.

No day goes by without a new crime.

Palestinian mothers, just like Iranian and American mothers, love their children, and are painfully bereaved by the imprisonment, wounding and murder of their children. What mother wouldn't?

For 60 years, the Zionist regime has driven millions of the inhabitants of Palestine out of their homes. Many of these refugees have died in the Diaspora and in refugee camps. Their children have spent their youth in these camps and are aging while still in the hope of returning to homeland.

You know well that the US administration has persistently provided blind and blanket support to the Zionist regime, has emboldened it to continue its crimes, and has prevented the UN Security Council from condemning it.

Who can deny such broken promises and grave injustices towards humanity by the US administration?

Governments are there to serve their own people. No people wants to side with or support any oppressors. But regrettably, the US administration disregards even its own public opinion and remains in the forefront of supporting the trampling of the rights of the Palestinian people.

Let's take a look at Iraq . Since the commencement of the US military presence in Iraq , hundreds of thousands of Iraqis have been killed, maimed or displaced. Terrorism in Iraq has grown exponentially. With the presence of the US military in Iraq , nothing has been done to rebuild the ruins, to restore the infrastructure or to alleviate poverty. The US Government used the pretext of the existence of weapons of mass destruction in Iraq , but later it became clear that that was just a lie and a deception.

Although Saddam was overthrown and people are happy about his departure, the pain and suffering of the Iraqi people has persisted and has even been aggravated.

In Iraq , about one hundred and fifty thousand American soldiers, separated from their families and loved ones, are operating under the command of the current US administration. A substantial number of them have been killed or wounded and their presence in Iraq has tarnished the image of the American people and government.

Their mothers and relatives have, on numerous occasions, displayed their discontent with the presence of their sons and daughters in a land thousands of miles away from US shores. American soldiers often wonder why they have been sent to Iraq .

I consider it extremely unlikely that you, the American people, consent to the billions of dollars of annual expenditure from your treasury for this military misadventure.

Noble Americans,

You have heard that the US administration is kidnapping its presumed opponents from across the globe and arbitrarily holding them without trial or any international supervision in horrendous prisons that it has established in various parts of the world. God knows who these detainees actually are, and what terrible fate awaits them.

You have certainly heard the sad stories of the Guantanamo and Abu-Ghraib prisons. The US administration attempts to justify them through its proclaimed "war on terror." But every one knows that such behavior, in fact, offends global public opinion, exacerbates resentment and thereby spreads terrorism, and tarnishes the US image and its credibility among nations.

The US administration's illegal and immoral behavior is not even confined to outside its borders. You are witnessing daily that under the pretext of "the war on terror," civil liberties in the United States are being increasingly curtailed. Even the privacy of individuals is fast losing its meaning. Judicial due process and fundamental rights are trampled upon. Private phones are tapped; suspects are arbitrarily arrested, sometimes beaten in the streets, or even shot to death.

I have no doubt that the American people do not approve of this behavior and indeed deplore it.

The US administration does not accept accountability before any organization, institution or council. The US administration has undermined the credibility of international organizations, particularly the United Nations and its Security Council. But, I do not intend to address all the challenges and calamities in this message.

The legitimacy, power and influence of a government do not emanate from its arsenals of tanks, fighter aircrafts, missiles or nuclear weapons. Legitimacy and influence reside in sound logic, quest for justice and compassion and empathy for all humanity. The global position of the United States is in all probability weakened because the administration has continued to resort to force, to conceal the truth, and to mislead the American people about its policies and practices.

Undoubtedly, the American people are not satisfied with this behavior and they showed their discontent in the recent elections. I hope that in the wake of the mid-term elections, the administration of President Bush will have heard and will heed the message of the American people.

My questions are the following:

Is there not a better approach to governance?

Is it not possible to put wealth and power in the service of peace, stability, prosperity and the happiness of all peoples through a commitment to justice and respect for the rights of all nations, instead of aggression and war?

We all condemn terrorism, because its victims are the innocent.

But, can terrorism be contained and eradicated through war, destruction and the killing of hundreds of thousands of innocents? If that were possible, then why has the problem not been resolved? The sad experience of invading Iraq is before us all.

What has blind support for the Zionists by the US administration brought for the American people? It is regrettable that for the US administration, the interests of these occupiers supersedes the interests of the American people and of the other nations of the world.

What have the Zionists done for the American people that the US administration considers itself obliged to blindly support these infamous aggressors? Is it not because they have imposed themselves on a substantial portion of the banking, financial, cultural and media sectors?

I recommend that in a demonstration of respect for the American people and for humanity, the right of Palestinians to live in their own homeland should be recognized so that millions of Palestinian refugees can return to their homes and the future of all of Palestine and its form of government be determined in a referendum. This will benefit everyone.

Now that Iraq has a Constitution and an independent Assembly and Government, would it not be more beneficial to bring the US officers and soldiers home, and to spend the astronomical US military expenditures in Iraq for the welfare and prosperity of the American people? As you know very well, many victims of Katrina continue to suffer, and countless Americans continue to live in poverty and homelessness.

I'd also like to say a word to the winners of the recent elections in the US :

The United States has had many administrations; some who have left a positive legacy, and others that are neither remembered fondly by the American people nor by other nations.

Now that you control an important branch of the US Government, you will also be held to account by the people and by history.

If the US Government meets the current domestic and external challenges with an approach based on truth and Justice, it can remedy some of the past afflictions and alleviate some of the global resentment and hatred of America . But if the approach remains the same, it would not be unexpected that the American people would similarly reject the new electoral winners, although the recent elections, rather than reflecting a victory, in reality point to the failure of the current administration's policies. These issues had been extensively dealt with in my letter to President Bush earlier this year.

To sum up:

It is possible to govern based on an approach that is distinctly different from one of coercion, force and injustice.

It is possible to sincerely serve and promote common human values, and honesty and compassion.

It is possible to provide welfare and prosperity without tension, threats, imposition or war.

It is possible to lead the world towards the aspired perfection by adhering to unity, monotheism, morality and spirituality and drawing upon the teachings of the Divine Prophets.

Then, the American people, who are God-fearing and followers of Divine religions, will overcome every difficulty.

What I stated represents some of my anxieties and concerns.

I am confident that you, the American people, will play an instrumental role in the establishment of justice and spirituality throughout the world. The promises of the Almighty and His prophets will certainly be realized; Justice and Truth will prevail and all nations will live a true life in a climate replete with love, compassion and fraternity.

The US governing establishment, the authorities and the powerful should not choose irreversible paths. As all prophets have taught us, injustice and transgression will eventually bring about decline and demise. Today, the path of return to faith and spirituality is open and unimpeded.

We should all heed the Divine Word

" But those who repent, have faith and do good may receive Salvation. Your Lord, alone, creates and chooses as He will, and others have no part in His choice; Glorified is God and Exalted above any partners they ascribe to Him. "

I pray to the Almighty to bless the Iranian and American nations and indeed all nations of the world with dignity and success.

POWERS GIVEN TO PRESIDENT BUSH, BY THIS 110TH CONGRESS;

Now, martial law can be declared not just for insurrection, but also for natural disasters, public health reasons, terrorist attacks or incidents, or for the vague reason called "other conditions." The President can call up the National Guard without congressional approval or the Governors' approval, and even send these State Guard troops into other States.

The American Republic is in remnant status. The stage is set for our country eventually revolving into a military dictatorship, and few seem to care. These precedent-setting changes in the law are extremely dangerous and will change American jurisprudence forever if not revised. The beneficial results of our revolt against the King's abuses are about to be eliminated, and few Members of Congress and few Americans are aware of the seriousness of the situation. Complacency and fear drive our legislation without any serious objection by our elected leaders. Sadly, though, those few who do object to this self-evident trend away from personal liberty and empire building overseas are portrayed as unpatriotic and uncaring.

...

Unsound policy can never help the troops. Keeping the troops out of harm's way and out of wars unrelated to our national security is the only real way of protecting the troops. With this understanding, just who can claim the title of "patriot"?

Before the war in the Middle East spreads and becomes a world conflict for which we will be held responsible, or the liberties of all Americans become so suppressed we can no longer resist, much has to be done. Time is short, but our course of action should be clear. Resistance to illegal and unconstitutional usurpation of our rights is required. Each of us must choose which course of action we should take: education, conventional political action, or even peaceful civil disobedience to bring about necessary changes.

But let it not be said that we did nothing. Let not those who love the power of the welfare/warfare state label the dissenters of authoritarianism as unpatriotic or uncaring. Patriotism is more closely linked to dissent than it is to conformity and a blind desire for safety and security. Understanding the magnificent rewards of a free society makes us untactful in its promotion, fully realizing that maximum wealth is created and the greatest chance for peace comes from a society respectful of individual liberty.

By now many Americans are aware that Israel, with a population of only 5.8 million people, is the largest recipient of U.S. foreign aid, and that Israel's aid plus U.S. aid to Egypt's 65 million people for keeping the peace with Israel has, for many years, consumed more than half of the U.S. bi-lateral foreign aid budget world-wide.

What few Americans understand however, is the steep price they pay in many other fields for the U.S.-Israeli relationship, which in turn is a product of the influence of Israel's powerful U.S. lobby on American domestic politics and has nothing to do with U.S. strategic interests, U.S. national interests, or even with traditional American support for self-determination, human rights, and fair play overseas.

Besides its financial cost, unwavering U.S. support for Israel, whether it's right or wrong, exacts a huge price in American prestige and credibility overseas. Further, Israel's powerful U.S. lobby has been a major factor in delaying campaign finance reform, and also in the removal from American political life of some of our most distinguished public servants, members of Congress and even presidents.

Finally, the Israel-U.S. relationship has cost a significant number of American lives. The incidents in which hundreds of U.S. service personnel, diplomats, and civilians have been killed in the Middle East have been reported in the media. But the media seldom revisits these events, and scrupulously avoids analyzing why they occurred or compiling the cumulative toll of American deaths resulting from our Israel-centered Middle East policies.

If the United States wants to win this war on terrorism then getting tough with Israel would be the best step they could take. Politically, it is a hard choice, but ultimately a sensible and realistic one that would bring about true peace and justice in the Middle East.

"Amidst all this violence and bloodshed" in Iraq, "is the sacrifice worth it?

Republican and Democrat congress alike know and could care less that the sacrifice is being borne overwhelmingly by lower-income whites, Hispanics and African-Americans who comprise the bulk of the casualties? Nor do they address 655,000
civilian Iraq's killed in this corrupt war.

To understate the case, neither the Democratic Party nor Republican Party seem to be serving the people of the United States as well as they could. This, too, might be a blessing because maybe it is now time for a legitimate centrist third party to be formed to take back our government from polarized politics, special interests, corrupt lobbyists and some of the worst elements of American society.

We can point to many officeholders, career politicians and people behind the scenes and see that there is a dark side to both major parties. There seems to be financial corruption, political corruption, even moral and spiritual corruption in both parties.

Each day it is more apparent that another political party is needed for the 2008 presidential and congressional elections. Neither the Democrats nor the Republicans have done anything to eliminate ``Government for Sale" lobbying and the PAC system. America has been sold out, look at the
recent bills on the WAR and IMMIGRATION.

No mention is made by either party of the $9 trillion national debt which consumes more and more tax dollars in interest every year, even if we succeeded in having a balanced budget. The gap in income is becoming wider between the ``corporate elite" and the vast majority of working men and women. Good jobs are being lost daily. The Wall Street Journal reports a new corporate layoff in almost every issue. It seems like government has been "outsourced" to a foreign lobby (AIPAC).

Free trade is a joke and has resulted in the loss of thousands of jobs. Taxpayer money is used to compensate for bad loans by global bankers to corrupt foreign governments.

The larger specialty groups like Veterans Organizations, Seniors Organizations, etc. that are treated like meat to be processed through the grinder, before and after their usefulness was done, need to remember that the reason they fought/worked was to save the rights and liberties of The People of America and their children. Instead, they dig for scraps of which they fought, from the tables of lying tyrants eating our peoples rightly deserved sustenance. There will not be rights for individuals, groups or segments until there are rights for all.

What Are You Waiting On? America needs you now. The Constitution needs you now. Our rights and liberties as free men, women and children of God/nature and evolution need you now.
The sad reality, it has already occurred, the 2000, and 2004 presidential elections were just that, we have been damned to tyranny for the last seven years. This country's righteous heritage is lost to all. .
The Constitution was the most empowering document the founders could muster in their best effort from the best minds of the time, perhaps in all time, regarding liberty and government. It has been called, generation upon generation throughout the world, the gold standard of rights and freedom for the people and their protection from the government. Yet, our current government of neo-cons, media and even some individuals call it outdated, irrelevant to current times, "a living constitution", and various other false interpretations and claims, and now swear their oaths of office to this bastardized constitution.

There is only one true interpretation of the Constitution, the historical background interpretation. The founders also made sure to leave hundreds upon hundreds of quotes and documents that readily show the intent of the text.

PROCTOLOGIST VIEW OF THE ELETUS PERFECT JUST PERFECT

VIEW OF THE GOVERNMENT FROM THE REAR!!

FROM A PROCTOLOGIST VIEW OF THE PRESENT USA GOVERNMENT:

There has never been a more perfect group of hemorrhoids gathered around the biggest elected rectum and vice anus in history.

All requires permanent specialized surgical removal. No matter how embarrassing it is to our society, the problems need to be quickly and appropriately dealt with. Otherwise the cancer involved will spread and destroy the whole body leading to death of all functions as previously known. (OUR FREEDOMS)

"EXIT" IS THE MANDATE. ALONG WITH "CUT & RUN"

We the American people, much to your dismay, have Voted, and the demand is for immediate change of direction. We have watched the killing of Palestinians, Lebanese, Jordanians, Egyptians, Syrians. Iraqis, and if not stopped, there will be an attack on Iran.

Israel has asked time and again for all the hatred there is toward them. They are the aggressor, and the transgressor of International Law, Western Democracy, and GODS Law.

We the American people agree with most members of the UN. Israel needs to be stopped in their tracks.

We have witnessed all the destruction done by Israel, created by Israel, and by a coalition of governess that has supported them, with-out support from the people of such coalition governments.

The destruction we have seen leaves us with the attitude, Let the enemies they created take care of business, With out interference.

They brag about how they have the USA in their palms. Well, they certainly do not. Let them pay the over-due cost, to their neighbors.

John Abizaid, an army general, expressed his views on the question of troop withdrawal to a congressional panel in Washington DC on Wednesday.

Carl Levin, the next chairman of the senate armed services committee, wants the Pentagon to start pulling troops out in four to six months.

"US interference in Iraq" has not helped the country move forward. We all know its time to leave.

Military leaders seem to support stay the course, like Some magic will happen. Magic will only happen when we leave, and with-draw Support for Israel's genocide of its neighbors. American citizens and voters understand. The only Reason why government officials don't seem to is. The corruption involved, campaign contributions, the closed door sessions where the "DEAL OR NO DEAL" MANIPULATION by IS CONCLUDED.

Where, other than Washington, DC, does price Gouging start. We the American people can no longer afford the price of "Government for Sale"..

So what do we do now, with the United States entwined with Israel even more closely than before in its confrontation with two successful religious nationalist movements, Hezbollah and Hamas? It would be sensible to open negotiations aimed at solidifying the control of these movements by moderates. Instead, all the indicators are that we intend to blindly stumble down the path to further confrontation, which is not in the interest of the United States.

Why this administration has been unconcerned about an exit strategy from Iraq from the very beginning. We won't be leaving. Once they conquer Iraq, the United States will create permanent military bases in that country from which to dominate the Middle East, including neighboring Iran.

Given history and the importance of Middle East oil, Iraq has become what Eqbal Ahmad used to call "the geopolitical center of the struggle for world power."

It is difficult to believe that with the U.S. establishment having all but conceded defeat in Iraq, and with the Baker-Hamilton Iraq Study Group having signaled that the United States needs the help of its rivals Iran and Syria – as well as Turkey, Saudi Arabia, and other influential Middle Eastern nations – to contain the Iraqi civil war, the U.S. and Israel are still pursuing the war and building permanent military bases in the disintegrating nation. Yet, this is precisely what the Pentagon is doing.

Whether the U.S. retains five or 15 "enduring bases," its goal is clear: to keep its military hand on the "jugular vein" of global capitalism – as former Joint Chiefs of Staff Chairman Maxwell Taylor described Middle East oil. This requires an intimidating infrastructure of deadly high-tech fortresses and the warriors that go with them.

All U.S. troops must be brought home if there is to be a chance for peace in Iraq. If the region's nations are to have any hope of finally exercising self-determination, and if the United States wants to regain the trust, and support of the international community, its military bases must be closed – quickly and permanently.

It all depends on how submissive the rest of the WORLD is. Right now there is no notable objection.

We want America to be the America we knew, Prior to the ambush by AIPAC and other such Foreign influences.

Will any of you stand up for the principles of Consequence and truth. Regardless, we Americans know the truth, and When you all decide to face it, do something about it. We then will be behind you 150 %, but until that, the Captain is going down with his ship. Mission accomplished or not.

IT IS UP TO YOU, IF YOU ALL STAY IN DENIAL!!

Declaration of Revolution:

The following is a Declaration of Revolution, brought forth by the people of this great land who were granted certain rights and freedoms under the Constitution. These rights and freedoms were brought to bear by our forefathers. They were defended with the blood of our soldiers. They have been kept sacred by the patriots of the past and present.

The United States Government is threatening to strip us of these rights and freedoms. Bills, such as the Patriot Act, have systematically dismantled and trampled upon our Constitution, thus dismantling the great republic we hold so dear. They have declared unjust wars, committed acts of tyranny, levied an unjust tax system, devalued our dollar and robbed good people of appropriate health care for decades.

We all face an uncertain future. For, without these rights and freedoms, the government possesses full control of us and our children. This cannot stand!

I hereby provide a list of demands brought forth by this Declaration of Revolution:

1. We demand a new, independent 9\11 Investigation - Nearly 3,000 innocent Americans lost their lives on September 11th, 2001. The official government account of the events has been proven false. We demand the truth!

2. We demand the shutdown of the Federal Reserve - We lost our rights of Taxation without Representation long ago. The Federal Reserve is a fraud. Not a single penny of our income tax goes to pay for federal programs. We demand answers!

3. We demand our freedom of speech - The First Amendment gives us the right to say what we want, where we want. The Government does not have the right to arrest us for expressing this right. This right is fundamental!

4. We demand our right to bear arms - Americans have the right to own guns. Taking away this right not only empowers criminals, it also strips away a fundamental right, known as the Second Amendment!

5. We demand impeachment and possible imprisonment of all current members of this government who have been involved in criminal activity - These citizens are not above the law and should be treated as equals. We demand justice!

6. We demand the withdrawal of all illegal occupations of foreign nations - The occupations of Iraq and Afghanistan have created tension and chaos and have lead to the deaths of hundreds of thousands of people around the world. These occupations also create an increased threat to the citizens of our country!

If these demands are not met within an appropriate amount of time, this Revolution may turn into a Resistance!

We demand our country back!

The Cronyism from the very beginning of the attack and invasion of Iraq still exist, and the profits from nothing done are still pouring into the pockets of the Corrupt. ANY official that is opposed to bringing home the troops has to be considering their own profits..

A tremendous amount of money on no bid contracts comes right back to this administration and members of congress.

The secretly arranged contracts, and profiteering, another part of the "organized crime" scheme. Six contractors gave millions to campaigns, 85% to the republican mob.

DEATH POEM
Take my blood.
Take my death shroud and
The remnants of my body.
Take photographs of my corpse at the grave, lonely.
Send them to the world,
To the judges and
To the people of conscience,
Send them to the principled men and the fair-minded.
And let them bear the guilty burden, before the world,
Of this innocent soul.
Let them bear the burden, before their children and before history,
Of this wasted, sinless soul,
Of this soul which has suffered at the hands of the "protectors of peace."

Many cultures, many ways of worship, many forms of religion. Christians such as myself believe in "Jesus" and the new Testament.

I pray to God in the name of Jesus:

I apologize for the crimes and actions of our, Government & officials,against other humans.

I ask for forgiveness for my sins, and pray that The suffering of the innocent, burden those responsible & guilty for ETERNITY.

We shall condemn the self-righteous hypocrites of false leadership and profiteers. All with ties to Bush/Cheney administration, Halliburton, Bechtel Group Inc, and several private security companies. Those companies conduct war of aggression. They are guns for hire, at a high profit for those involved. Torture at prisons, intelligence gathering? stalking the citizens carrying machine guns, they are paid to train Iraqi's, kill others, and are a ubiquitous and offensive symbol of the US occupation. These guerillas make up more then 25% of the occupation force in Iraq. Heavily armed mercenaries are paid several times more than our troops.

You need to know that they, unlike our military in Iraq, have complete immunity issued by the US Coalition. They perform the aggression Bush/Cheney wants, crucial military jobs once entrusted to the military. They guard the US officials, and key locations in Iraq. Why!! Seems they do not have to answer to the congress or any law. 25% of the money being spent goes to these security companies. Blackwell, best known has 450 personnel, some at $1,500 a day. Blackwater also employs 60 Chilean ex-commandos who were trained under the Pinochet dictatorship.

The American firm DynCorp has a $50 million contract to train Iraqi police officers.

The firm USA Environmental has teams of weapons and explosive experts in Iraq and a $65 million contract to collect and destroy unexploded ordinance. Vinnell, a subsidiary of Northman Grumman, has a $48 million contract to assist in the training of a new Iraqi Army. Erinys has the $100 million-plus annual contract to provide security at Iraq's oil facilities and pipelines. Erinys employs some 14,000 Iraqi security guards on wages of $150 per month, supervised by dozens of former British and apartheid-era South African military. The secrecy surrounding the operations is enabling the White House to obscure the actual cost in terms of men and casualties it is taking to sustain the illegal occupation of Iraq.

Together six of the many companies contracted in Iraq contributed $3.6 million to federal election campaigns, 85% to Republicans,

119

according to the Center for Responsive Politics. HOW MUCH more from others is still a secret?

Call it what it is favoritism, collusion, and war profiteering. WE SUPPORT OUR TROOPS, BRING THEM HOME.

Ask why no over-site, no accountability. WHO is profiting from the losses. 3800 killed. THOUSANDS wounded. (American troops) 700,000 Iraqi civilians killed, thousands wounded, millions relocated.

This has not been to liberate. It is to occupy and profit.

NOW, will you get angry with the rest of us? Is this what you neo-cons jumped in for? Is this your faith at work?? Do you support this profiteering by organized crime, Bush/Cheney & friends?

As you may correctly assume, we have become high mileage, and been to a few local, county, state plus other fairs.

I hope to share those experiences in the future

TO BE CONTINUED:

PS: Letter to me from: Barrack Obama

Dear Ronald,

House built on a strong foundation should withstand floods and high winds.
A government built on a strong foundation of solidarity and common purpose should aid its citizens when their houses are not strong enough.
Two years ago, Hurricane Katrina revealed that our federal emergency response system and the leadership responsible for it lacked a strong foundation.

As thousands drowned and lost their homes, President Bush and FEMA responded incompetently to this tragedy.

Over the weeks and months that followed, things at FEMA didn't get much better. There's been a lot of squabbling, but no one has stepped up to take responsibility.

Nonetheless, New Orleans and other communities on the Gulf Coast are making a recovery -- small businesses, neighborhoods, and churches are coming back to life thanks to individuals and organizations taking matters into their own hands. In the absence of proper support from the federal government, Americans have reached out to one another and begun the work that the Bush administration has neglected.

Those working on the recovery have honored a principle our government has largely forgotten under President Bush: I am my brother's keeper, I am my sister's keeper.

Yet even for patient and generous people, the burdens continue to be overwhelming.

There are countless problems remaining to be solved: shuttered schools and hospitals, abandoned houses, faulty levees, and more empty promises from Washington.

New Orleans and the whole Gulf Coast face huge challenges ahead. But rebuilding is also an opportunity.

In rebuilding, we've got a chance to create something stronger -- a foundation that can serve as the rock on which dreams are founded. Our focus should be on strengthening the fundamental elements any community needs to thrive: maintaining local law and order, bringing doctors and nurses back to provide reliable healthcare, and attracting top teachers to restore schools that will give our children the chance to succeed.

But to do this we must change our leadership.

These failures expose arrogance in our current leaders -- a detachment from the lives of real people and an indifference to the consequences for the least fortunate -- that cannot continue.

And make no mistake; the failures of the Bush administration were not just failures of response. They were the end result of policies that have eroded our country's foundation and weakened our commitment to one another.

To rebuild in the wake of Katrina and get our country back on course, we need to renew our commitment to one another. We need to return to this core principle of our great nation by honoring our responsibility to our fellow citizens.

I am my brother's keeper. I am my sister's keeper. And that foundation is what makes all of us stronger.

Thank you.

Barack Obama

P.S. -- You don't have to wait for a new president to be elected to do something right now to help speed the recovery of the Gulf Coast.

Since the storms of 2005, Habitat for Humanity has increased its production of homes for those in need more than tenfold. Please consider supporting the recovery by donating to or volunteering for Habitat for Humanity.

Habit for Humanity is where I donate, how about you doing the same!!

Ron Waldron

September 7, 2007

An Open Letter to All of the Candidates Running in the 2008 Election

Dear Sirs and Madam,

What has amazed me over the last several months of watching you as you run for the highest office in the land. The opportunity to serve as the head CEO of the Corporation of the United States of America, is that not one of you has set down to write a complete proposal to the people of what it is that you would intend to do while serving in this vital position.

In order to graduate from any one of our fine educational institutions you would be expected to write a paper of some kind on some area of learned knowledge but here in the case of running for this top position you don't feel that there is any real need to do so.

I disagree with you completely, I feel we the people who are being asked to hire you have a right and you have an obligation to prepare for us a complete Proposal, what work you intend to do, where you intend to get the money that you would need to set into progress the things that you intend to achieve and any time lines that you would set for achieving these goals so that we would know if the government actually is making any progress on it's benchmarks. How you intend to work with Senators, Representatives, as well as Governors and Mayors to achieve the goals that you have set out for yourself on behalf of those you SERVE.

To date I have heard clever rhetorical responses, some of which I might be able to agree, some not. However, in order to determine who has the best overall plan that we the people can actually afford to place into effect I have seen no evidence. Mostly a bunch of promises made to placate the audience at hand.

This country is at too pivotal a time in its history for simple platitudes. The problems that we face are many and large and costly. It is essential that an honest and thorough dialogue begin in order that the people can make wise choices, not those that are only based on their own limited self interests and this must include the narrow interests of Corporations.

When I hire someone to do work in my home I generally get Proposals from different Contactors, which include the work they intend to do the time at which they expect that I give them a certain amount of money for equipment, labor and then completion of the work. There are also clauses that penalize the contractor for not meeting deadlines as well as quality assurances as defined in the proposal. Why should I expect something less from you?

I am tired of a government that is being run inefficiently without any accountability. The government is not your own little play yard that allows you do as you please, you have responsibilities to the people that sent you there to represent them. It would be much easier to see if you were achieving your goals if said goals were laid out in an orderly and succinct manner.

Please do not misunderstand me I realize that the job is a difficult undertaking and can not for life of me understand why so many of you want the job. I t doesn't even pay that well although the perks are pretty good.

I have had an opportunity to read some of your views on foreign policy, pretty much excluding all areas other than the Middle East. Which in my mind is a limited discussion on a topic which considering the Global nature of our world today is simply insufficient. There also needs to be a broader discussion on the domestic front as well, the problems are large, costly and many.

What we need is a written PRPOPOSAL given to us in a timely fashion that will allow us to read it over and then mull it over from each of you in your own words. You do not need to waste your limited or unlimited resources by polling. I myself will never tell anyone in advance of voting how I will vote as I DO BELIEVE IN THE SECRET BALLOT.

I realize that this letters' length lends it to not being read. I'm not sure why, whether it's due to your short attention spans or that your just to busy to listen to the people whom you would like to vote you into office. In either case I will post it for others to read, so perhaps my views will be heard by someone even if not by those who should damn well be listening.

If lawmakers don't act with clarity and conviction in the weeks ahead, this Congress, headed by House Speaker Nancy Pelosi and Senate Leader Harry Reid, will be remembered as the Congress that failed freedom. We can't let that happen.
Each and every one of us must remain outspoken and vigilant. It's going to be a fight to get this Congress to conduct real oversight and restore our Constitution. But with your help, we can get it done.
Subject: TURMOIL OVER COURT APPOINTMENT

Since the election fraud of 2000, the American people have been in turmoil over the appointment.

An explanation should be in order.

Did the court appoint a President, Dictator, Reverend, Rabbi, or organized crime chief to preside at our White House? Or has the office become one and the same?

We have no questions on our minds that you appointed the "Underground Worlds" --God-Father" as vice president.

Is our government now exclusive to the Executive, Legislative, or Judicial Branch or have all three merged at the Oval office?

We realize that all of you receive large checks from our tax base, and from every lobby in this world.

How-ever is there anyone working for the interest of America? It seems, do to the diligence of AIPAC, Israel is now the only beneficiary of such maneuvering, and the only real recipient of any effort by OUR government.

Such seems to be the consequences of another merger, the merger of Church & State. Of course such merger did not include moral values, ethics, or integrity. And is very evident it is the Axis of Evil.

Bush's Wiretaps: Impeachment not Immunity Two years ago, the NY Times revealed George Bush has been illegally wiretapping our phones and emails for years. Bush publicly admitted signing the authorizations for illegal wiretaps over 30 times.

Bush's warrantless wiretaps are a flagrant violation of the Fourth Amendment. And under the 1978 FISA law, the penalty for each of Bush's illegal wiretaps is up to $10,000 and 5 years in prison. Bush may have wiretapped millions of Americans, so he should not only be impeached, but he should spend the rest of his life behind bars.

On Tuesday's Ed Schultz Show, Nancy Pelosi struggled to explain why she opposes impeaching Bush and Cheney. She said if anyone could prove Bush committed impeachable offenses, they should contact her.

Of course violating the Fourth Amendment and FISA is impeachable, and it's proved by Bush's confession (see above). Rewriting laws with signing statements is impeachable, and it's proved by the statements posted on the White House website and by a GAO study finding that in many cases Bush has proceeded to violate the laws he claims the right to violate. Refusing to comply with subpoenas is impeachable, and there is no dispute that Bush and Cheney have refused to comply.

The evidence collected at http://www.afterdowningstreet

Ten Reasons to Impeach George Bush and Dick Cheney

I ask Congress to impeach President Bush and Vice President Cheney for the following reasons:

1. Violating the United Nations Charter by launching an illegal "War of Aggression" against Iraq without cause, using fraud to sell the war to Congress and the public, misusing government funds to begin bombing without Congressional authorization, and subjecting our military personnel to unnecessary harm, debilitating injuries, and deaths.

2. Violating U.S. and international law by authorizing the torture of thousands of captives, resulting in dozens of deaths, and keeping prisoners hidden from the International Committee of the Red Cross.

3. Violating the Constitution by arbitrarily detaining Americans, legal residents, and non-Americans, without due process, without charge, and without access to counsel.

4. Violating the Geneva Conventions by targeting civilians, journalists, hospitals, and ambulances, and using illegal weapons, including white phosphorous, depleted uranium, and a new type of napalm.

5. Violating U.S. law and the Constitution through widespread wiretapping of the phone calls and emails of Americans without a warrant.

6. Violating the Constitution by using "signing statements" to defy hundreds of laws passed by Congress.

7. Violating U.S. and state law by obstructing honest elections in 2000, 2002, 2004, and 2006.

8. Violating U.S. law by using paid propaganda and disinformation, selectively and misleadingly leaking classified information, and exposing the identity of a covert CIA operative working on sensitive WMD proliferation for political retribution.

9. Subverting the Constitution and abusing Presidential power by asserting a "Unitary Executive Theory" giving unlimited powers to the President, by obstructing efforts by Congress and the Courts to review and restrict Presidential actions, and by promoting and signing legislation negating the Bill of Rights and the Writ of Habeas Corpus.

10. Gross negligence in failing to assist New Orleans residents after Hurricane Katrina, in ignoring urgent warnings of an Al Qaeda attack prior to Sept. 11, 2001, and in increasing air pollution causing global warming.

By refusing to allow Saddam to flee with guarantees, Bush ensured that a land war would have to be fought. This is one of the greatest crimes any US president ever committed, and it is all the more contemptible for being rooted in mere pride and petulance.
He had a real offer in the hand, of Saddam's flight. He rejected it. By rejecting it, he will have killed at least a million persons and became one of the more monstrous figures in recent world history.

Now it is time for the American people to go to war against the FASCISM, of this our present form of government, that has assumed power over us..

The real problem with America is who is in the White House, a ventriloquist dummy who has spent 6 plus years being manipulated by Dick Cheney. Not only can NO progress be made on any issue until they are removed, unless they are impeached the amount of additional havoc they will wreck in the next 500 days is too terrible to contemplate.

In America those believing they are born to rule behave with such brutality to defend their rights, their property, their hold over society that they approach true fascism (This Administration..)

Subject: A COUP HAS OCCURRED!!

GOVERNMENT SOLD, NOT FOR SALE. FOREIGN POLICY IS ISRAEL & AIPAC CONTROLLED NO MATTER, WHO IS IN OFFICE.

OUR GOVERNMENT IS NOT FOR-SALE, IT HAS BEEN SOLD:

More then 150 million dollars have been raised from the American People, for the Democratic Party on lies to end the WAR.

This time it isn't the republicans telling the lies, it is all top 3 democrat candidates for the Democrat Party. Time after time, the deception has been, vote for me, and give me money I will immediately Leave IRAQ. The first thing to be done is BRING OUR TROOPS HOME. Not even redeploy. The claim was BRING THEM HOME.

Now after raising record amounts from individual Americans, we hear a different story. One that shows how special interest groups, foreign lobbies dictate to all parties. Republican, Democrat No longer matters.

Now to realize that the Fascist coupe, that has occurred, is a take over of both parties, Of both houses, now it does not matter. No one takes a second look at impeachment, or to hold ANYONE accountable.

It is a sad state of affairs. America no longer has a real choice. We vote only as an impudent citizen. Our choice is based on, vote for a female, vote for a black, vote for a conservative, vote for a liberal, Vote for an actor, but the REAL ISSUES for AMERICA are off the TABLE,

IMPEACHMENT, WAR, HEALTH CARE, IMMIGRATION, BORDER CONTROL, OUT-SOURCING, FOREIGN TRADE, REAL CAMPAIGN REFORM, CHECKS & BALANCE, CENSORSHIP, CONSTITUTIONAL VIOLATIONS, PRIVATE ARMIES, HUMAN RIGHTS, LOBBIES, EVERY ISSUE SEEMS TO BE A VIOLATION OF SOME HATE

CRIME. ALL MOSTLY CALLED, ANTI-SEMENTIC. NOW WE FACE A GLOBAL ANTI-SEMENTIC LAW. LOBBIED AND PAID FOR BY ISRAEL & AIPAC.

Talk about Arrogance! Bush signs a law judging the rest of the world. While Bush ignores the ruling of the UN and the World Court! It's not even a good law! That's why the world needs a bipartisan world rather than one superpower. The power goes into their head!

The world does not exist for Jews and Israel only, but all of our policies and new laws, and most decisions are now made with their interest in mind only. WHY IS THAT!!!

Americans need to revolt. We are losing all.

Read: President Jimmy Carter's book. Read: Professor's John Mearsheimer & Steven Walt. Read: Richard Clark's book. Read & Listen: To weapons inspector Scott Ritter.

How about a panel of these individuals, not Media personalities, or other special interest personalities, let them voice what is going on, what needs to be done, And most important what candidate, OR candidates they would endorse IF ANY. The changes that need to be made IMMEDIATELY.

That is because two things come together that with the acceptance for various reasons of the Congress – Democrats and Republicans – and the public and the media, we have freed the White House – the president and the vice president – from virtually any restraint by Congress, courts, media, public, whatever.

And on the other hand, the people who have this unrestrained power are crazy."

'A Coup Has Occurred'

Bush and Cheney have been subverting our Constitution since they took office. They've also been undermining the basic principles on which America was founded, the principles of liberty, equality and justice for all. They've corrupted Congress, taken over the mainstream media to use as their propaganda organ, used the military to further their private interests, drained the treasury, hastened environmental catastrophe, and terrorized the population with rumors of false flag operations, bird flu epidemics, concentration camps meant for us, etc, etc, etc. Cheney has issued veiled hints about nuking an American city- the internet is buzzing with concern about the missing nuclear-tipped cruise missile.

It's now clear that from the start, the goal of Bush and Cheney has been to create the conditions necessary to institute a dictatorship.

Subject: ISRAELI LOBBY

Breaking the taboo: why we took on the Israel lobby
By: John Mearsheimer, Stephen Walt
Truthdig.com
4 October 2007

http://www.truthdig.com/interview/item/20071004_breaking_the_taboo_why_we_took_on_the_israel_lobby/
Eric Chinski, the editor of John J. Mearsheimer and Stephen M. Walt's provocative new bestseller, asks the authors whether their book is good for the Jews and good for America. This interview originally appeared on the Web site of the publishing house Farrar, Straus and Giroux.

Why did your article "The Israel Lobby," which was published in the London Review of Books in 2006, provoke such heated discussion around the world? James Traub wrote in The New York Times Magazine: " 'The Israel Lobby' slammed into the opinion-making world with a Category 5 force." How would you describe the reaction?

The article received enormous attention because it challenged what had become a taboo issue in mainstream foreign policy circles, namely the impact of the Israel lobby on U.S. Middle East policy. We did not question Israel's legitimacy and explicitly stated that the United States should come to Israel's aid if its survival is at risk, but we did argue that pro-Israel groups in the United States were encouraging policies that were ultimately not in America's national interest. Although the views we expressed are often discussed openly in other democracies—including Israel itself—they have rarely been set forth in detail by mainstream figures in the United States. The article was also of great interest to many readers because it has become increasingly obvious that U.S. Middle East policy has gone badly awry. Although a number of groups and individuals either mischaracterized our views or attacked us personally, many other readers agreed that such an examination of the lobby's role was long overdue.

Why did you feel the need to follow up the article with your book "The Israel Lobby and U.S. Foreign Policy"? What more is there to say?

Writing a book provided an opportunity to present a more nuanced and complete statement of our views, and also allowed us to address some of the responses to the original article. Although the article was long by magazine standards, space limitations forced us to omit several key issues and to deal with other topics more briefly than we would have liked. Events like the 2006 Lebanon war had not occurred when the article was published, and additional information about other episodes—such as the U.S. decision to invade Iraq—had since come to light. Thus, writing a book allowed us to refine our analysis and bring it up to date.

In particular, the book presents a more detailed definition of the lobby, an extended discussion of its development and rightward drift over time, an examination of the role of the so-called Christian Zionists, and an analysis of the controversial issue of "dual loyalty." We also offer a more detailed description of the various strategies that groups in the lobby use to advance their goals within the U.S. political system. The book also addresses the widespread belief—as illustrated by Michael Moore's documentary "Fahrenheit 9/11"— that oil companies are the real driving force behind America's Middle East policy, and explains why this view is incorrect.

Finally, our original article did not offer much in the way of positive prescriptions, but the book outlines a new approach to U.S. Middle East policy that would better serve U.S. interests and, in our view, be better for Israel as well. To that end, it also identifies how the influence of the lobby might become more constructive, for the good of both countries.

What is the extent of American financial, diplomatic, and military aid to Israel, and how does it compare with other states'?

Israel is the largest recipient of U.S. economic and military assistance, having received more than $154 billion in U.S. aid since its creation in 1948, and it currently receives roughly $3 billion in direct U.S. assistance every year, even though it is now a prosperous country. The United States also consistently gives Israel diplomatic support, and consistently comes to its aid in wartime, as it did during the 2006 war in Lebanon. Most important, U.S. support for Israel is largely unconditional: Israel receives generous American assistance even when it takes actions that the U.S. government believes are wrong, such as building settlements in the Occupied Territories. As former Prime Minister Yitzhak Rabin once remarked, U.S. backing for Israel is "beyond compare in modern history."

Isn't America's special relationship with Israel based on strong strategic and moral arguments? Isn't it important for the United States to have an ally that shares our values in a region dominated by extremism and enemies of America?

Israel is not the strategic asset to the United States that many claim. Israel may have been a strategic asset during the Cold War, but it has become a growing liability now that the Cold War is over. Unconditional support for Israel has reinforced anti-Americanism around the world, helped fuel America's terrorism problem, and strained relations with other key allies in Europe, the Middle East, and Asia. The United States derives some tangible strategic benefits from its close security partnership with Israel, but it pays a high price for them. On balance, it is more of a liability than an asset.

Similarly, the moral case for unconditional U.S. support is not compelling. Israel is a democracy, but no other democracy gets the same level of support that Israel does—and so unconditionally. There is a strong moral case for Israel's existence, which is why we support a Jewish state in Palestine and believe the U.S. should come to its aid if its survival is jeopardized. But many of Israel's policies—especially the continued occupation of the West Bank and its refusal to allow the Palestinians a viable state of their own—are at odds with key U.S. values. Viewed objectively, the early Zionists' behavior during the founding of the Jewish state and Israel's later behavior toward the Palestinians and its Arab neighbors undermine the myth of Israel as victim and the Arabs as aggressors.

The strategic and moral rationales for unconditional U.S. support have grown weaker since the end of the Cold War, yet U.S. support has continued to increase. This anomaly suggests that some other factor is at work.

Why do you focus on Israel and not on other U.S. allies?

We focus on Israel's policies in this book not because we have any animus toward Israel or because we regard its behavior as worse than other states'. Rather, we focus on it because the United States has long focused so much of its financial, diplomatic, and military attention on Israel. Israel is often said to deserve this support because it supposedly acts better than other states do, but we show that this is not the case. It has not acted worse than other states, but neither has it acted significantly better. Regrettably, uncritical U.S. support has led to policies that are harmful to the United States and Israel alike.

If the strategic and moral rationales don't account for the exceptional backing of Israel, what does?

The pro-Israel lobby. The lobby is a loose coalition of individuals and groups that actively works to push American policy in ways that will benefit Israel. It is not a cabal or conspiracy, or a single, hierarchical organization with a central leadership and total unanimity of views. Rather, it is a set of groups and individuals who all favor steadfast U.S. support for Israel but sometimes disagree on certain policy issues. Prominent groups in the lobby include the American Israel Public Affairs Committee (AIPAC), the Conference of Presidents of Major American Jewish Organizations, the Anti-Defamation League (ADL); Christians United for Israel (CUFI), and pro-Israel think tanks like the Washington Institute for Near East Policy and the American Enterprise Institute (AEI). Leading individuals in the lobby include the heads of these various organizations, as well as neoconservatives who served in the Bush administration like Elliott Abrams, John Bolton, Douglas Feith, Paul Wolfowitz, and David Wurmser, some of whom are closely associated with hard-line pro-Israel think tanks and conservative politicians in Israel, or Christian Zionists like John Hagee of CUFI and ... Tom DeLay (R-Texas).

Religious and ethnic identity does not define who is part of the lobby, as it includes gentiles as well as Jewish-Americans. It is the political agenda of an individual or a group, not ethnicity or religion, that determines whether they are part of the lobby. Thus, the Israel lobby is not synonymous with American Jewry, and "Jewish lobby" is not an appropriate term for describing the various groups and individuals that work to foster U.S. support for Israel. These groups and individuals sometimes disagree on particular issues but they are united in their belief that the "special relationship" between the United States and Israel should not be substantively questioned. They are not all-powerful and they do not "control" U.S. foreign policy. Rather, they form a powerful special interest group, which over time has acquired considerable influence over U.S. policy in the Middle East.

What are the strategies the lobby uses to influence the policymaking process and public discourse about Israel and its relationship with the United States?

The Israel lobby uses the same basic strategies that other interest groups employ. It pushes its agenda in Congress by supporting friendly candidates and legislators with votes and campaign money and by helping to frame legislation; by getting sympathetic individuals appointed to key policy positions in the executive branch; by monitoring the media and pressuring news organizations to offer favorable coverage; and by writing articles, books, and op-eds designed to move public opinion in directions they favor. These various strategies are as American as apple pie, and there is nothing illegitimate about them. Yet it ought to be equally legitimate to examine and discuss how the Israel lobby works to push its agenda in government, and to debate whether its influence is beneficial, the same way that one might examine other interest groups like the gun lobby, the farm lobby, the pharmaceutical lobby, the energy lobby, and other ethnic lobbies (e.g., Cuban-Americans, Indian-Americans, Armenian-Americans, etc.).

Do you think the Israel lobby's tactics sometimes go beyond acceptable interest-group politics?

Unfortunately, yes. Although most of the lobby's tactics are legitimate forms of political participation, some groups and individuals in the lobby also try to silence or marginalize opponents and critics by smearing them as anti-Semites or self-hating Jews. This sort of response was evident in the personal attacks directed at Jimmy Carter for writing a controversial book about Israeli policy in the Occupied Territories, and in the efforts of the American Jewish Committee and the Anti-Defamation League to prevent the historian Tony Judt from giving a lecture on the Israel lobby to a group in New York City. True anti-Semitism is loathsome and should be firmly opposed, but using this sort of accusation to silence or marginalize critics is antithetical to the principles of free speech and open debate on which democracy depends.

Why is it so difficult to talk about the role of the Israel lobby?

Primarily because of the many centuries of anti-Semitism in the Christian West, which culminated in the horrors of the Nazi Holocaust. Given this long history of sometimes violent persecution, Jewish Americans (and many gentiles) are understandably sensitive to any argument that is critical of Israel or of the political influence of groups in which Jews are central participants. This sensitivity is compounded by the memory of bizarre conspiracy theories of the sort laid out in "The Protocols of the Elders of Zion," a notorious anti-Semitic tract that was discredited long ago. Such paranoid views remain a staple of neo-Nazis and other fringe groups, however, which reinforces Jewish sensitivities even more. Given this history, some people are likely to suspect that anyone who criticizes Israel is in fact questioning its right to exist, or that anyone who examines the political influence of the Israel lobby is questioning the loyalty of pro-Israel individuals or accusing them of some sort of illegitimate activity. We explicitly reject these anti-Semitic notions, but given past experience, we understand why it is easier to talk about the influence of other special interest groups than it is to talk about the Israel lobby.

What is the lobby's impact on U.S. foreign policy in the Middle East?

In Part II of the book, we show how the lobby has encouraged the United States to take Israel's side in its long struggle with the Palestinians, and made it more difficult for the United States to help bring this conflict to a close. The lobby—and especially the neoconservatives within it—also played a key role in the decision to invade Iraq in 2003, although other factors (such as the September 11 attacks) were also critical in making the decision for war. The lobby has successfully pressed the Bush administration to adopt a more confrontational stance toward Syria and Iran, and encouraged it to back Israel to the hilt during the 2006 war in Lebanon.

Why are these policies not in America's national interest?

Backing Israel's harsh treatment of the Palestinians has reinforced anti-Americanism around the world and almost certainly helped terrorists recruit new followers. U.S. and Israeli policy also led directly to Hamas' growing popularity and its victory in the Palestinian elections, which made a difficult situation worse and a long-term peace settlement even more elusive. The Iraq war is a strategic disaster that has damaged America's standing and strengthened Iran's regional position, and now provides other terrorists with an ideal training ground. The Lebanon war enhanced Hezbollah's position, weakened the pro-American Siniora government in Beirut, and further tarnished America's image throughout the region. A hard-line approach to Iran helped bring President Mahmoud Ahmadinejad to power but failed to halt Iran's nuclear ambitions, and threatening Syria led Damascus to stop helping the United States against al Qaeda. None of these developments has been good for the United States.

What is the impact on Israel's long-term interests?

U.S. aid has indirectly subsidized Israel's attempt to colonize the Occupied Territories, a policy that many Israelis now see as a strategic and moral disaster. Yet the lobby has made it effectively impossible for Washington to convince the Israeli government to abandon this misguided policy. The lobby's influence has also made it harder for the United States to persuade Israel to seize opportunities—such as a peace treaty with Syria, the 2002 Saudi peace initiative, or full and complete implementation of the Oslo agreements—that would have saved Israeli lives and shrunk the number of enemies it still faces. The invasion of Iraq—which Israel and the lobby both supported— turned out to be a major boon for Iran, the country many Israelis fear most. And by pressing Congress and the Bush administration to back Israel's ill-conceived response to Hezbollah in the summer of 2006, the lobby unwittingly facilitated a policy that damaged Israel significantly.

Do you think the upcoming 2008 presidential campaign will provide a chance for the Israel lobby's influence to be discussed?

Regrettably, no. The candidates will undoubtedly disagree on a wide array of domestic and foreign-policy issues: health care, education, taxes, the environment, what to do in Iraq, how to deal with a rising China, etc. But the one issue on which there will be virtually no debate is the question of whether the United States should continue to give Israel unconditional backing. Even though almost everyone recognizes that U.S Middle East policy is a disaster, no serious candidate is going to suggest anything other than steadfast and largely unconditional support for Israel. Indeed, all the major candidates (Clinton, Edwards, McCain, Obama, Romney, etc.) have already expressed their strong and uncritical backing for Israel, even though the campaign is just getting underway. Not only is this situation bad for the United States, it is also not good for Israel. The United States would be a better ally if its leaders could make support for Israel more conditional and if they could give their Israeli counterparts more candid and critical advice without facing a backlash from the Israel lobby.

What in your view should the U.S.-Israel relationship look like? What should the lobby's role be?

The United States has three strategic interests in the Middle East: maintaining the flow of Persian Gulf oil to world markets, discouraging the spread of WMD, and reducing anti-American terrorism from this region. It is also committed to Israel's survival, but on moral rather than strategic grounds. Instead of garrisoning the region with its own troops or attempting to transform the entire region, the United States should act as an "offshore balancer." The United States does not need to control the Middle East itself; it merely needs to prevent any hostile power(s) from controlling the region. To do that, Washington should strive to maintain a balance of power in the region and intervene with its own forces only when local actors cannot uphold the balance themselves, as it did when it liberated Kuwait in 1991.

As part of this strategy, the United States would begin to treat Israel like a normal state, rather than as the 51st state. Israel is nearly 60 years old, increasingly prosperous, and now officially recognized by the vast majority of the world's nations. The United States should deal with it as it does with other democracies: backing Israel when its policies are consistent with U.S. interests, but opposing it when they are not. And the United States should use its considerable leverage to fashion a durable two-state solution, as it is the only outcome that is consistent with U.S. values and with the long-term interests of both America and Israel.

Achieving this shift will require overcoming the opposition from the most powerful groups in the lobby, like AIPAC and the Conference of Presidents. This goal can be achieved if there is a more open debate about the lobby's role in shaping U.S. policy, more widespread awareness of Israel's history and behavior, and a candid discussion within America's pro-Israel community. Instead of trying to weaken or counter the lobby, one may hope that moderate pro-Israel organizations will become more influential, and that the leading organizations realize that the hard-line positions they have espoused in the past have been counterproductive. If these groups can bring their impressive influence to bear in more constructive ways, U.S. policy will be more in line with its national interests, and better for Israel too.

ISRAEL IS THE ONLY MIDDLE EAST COUNTRY TO POSSESS WEAPONS OF MASS DISTRUCTION:

ISRAEL & THE USA FEAR TERRORISM. The Arab League fears the WMD of Israel & the USA..

Based on all the attacks & history of occupation, and Human Rights violations, of Israel on all its neighbors, why wouldn't other countries want to be able to defend themselves. They know that every time the international community tries to rein in Israel. The big brother imperialist ally, the USA, objects and vetos any and all resolutions.

On top of that, ignor the proliferation of such, and supplies Israel with missiles, war heads, and exaggerated amounts of foreign aid.

Syria, Iran, Lebanon, Egypt, Jordan, Libya, Turkey, and Saudi, in fact all members of the Arab League of Nations need to have great concerns, and should be taking immediate actions while they are able.

Israel has not confirmed that it has nuclear weapons and officially maintains that it will not be the first country to introduce nuclear weapons into the Middle East. Yet the existence of Israeli nuclear weapons is a "public secret" by now due to the declassification of large numbers of formerly highly classified US government documents which show that the United States by 1975 was convinced that Israel had nuclear weapons.

Although the United States government did not encourage or approve of the Israeli nuclear program, it also did nothing to stop it.

In early 1968, the CIA issued a report concluding that Israel had successfully started production of nuclear weapons.

It is also reported that, fearing defeat in the October 1973 Yom Kippur War, the Israelis assembled 13 twenty-kiloton atomic bombs.

By the late 1990s the U.S. Intelligence Community estimated that Israel possessed between 75-130 weapons, based on production estimates. The stockpile would certainly include warheads for mobile Jericho-1 and Jericho-2 missiles, as well as bombs for Israeli aircraft, and may include other tactical nuclear weapons of various types. Some published estimates even claimed that Israel might have as many as 400 nuclear weapons by the late 1990s.

The key variable that is specific to Israel is the power level of the reactor, which is reported to be at least 75 MWt and possibly as high as 200 MWt. New high-resolution satellite imagery provides important insight this matter. The imagery of the Dimona nuclear reactor was acquired by the Public Eye Project of the Federation of American Scientists from Space Imaging Corporation's IKONOS satellite. The cooling towers associated with the Dimona reactor are clearly visible and identifiable in satellite imagery.

This would suggest an annual production rate of plutonium of about 20 kilograms.

Based on plausible upper and lower bounds of the operating practices at the reactor, Israel could have thus produced enough plutonium for at least 100 nuclear weapons, but probably not significantly more than 200 weapons.
Israel controls American Government now, it won't be long globalization will be their control.
Israel is not the strategic asset to the United States that many claim. Israel may have been a strategic asset during the Cold War, but it has become a growing liability now that the Cold War is over. Unconditional support for Israel has reinforced anti-Americanism around the world, helped fuel America's terrorism problem, and strained relations with other key allies in Europe, the Middle East, and Asia. The United States derives some tangible strategic benefits from its close security partnership with Israel, but it pays a high price for them. On balance, it is more of a liability than an asset.

Subject: YOU CAN LEAD A HORSE TO WATER, BUT YOU CAN NOT MAKE IT DRINK!!

THE USA HAS SPENT BILLIONS training Iraqi's to kill, giving them all the advanced weaponry, and equipment, provided all necessary supplies. But they can not Americanize them. They will not TURN on their own civilian population. Time after time the trained units have turned against the coalition, rather then attack their own people.

To our government officials that seems strange, they do it all the time for money, power, and fame. How can any culture have a conviction of pride, moral values, integrity, ethics, over wealth. To value their own people over Imperialism, and control. Of course that was the regime they wanted to be liberated from, but now find them occupied by a "WAR" machine, a mechanism for profit, regardless of the death toll, or the suffering , and displacement of an entire population. A Christian nation was relied on, the Bible thumpers were believed. Now after total devastation of their country, they see the hypocrisy of it all. The lies to them, the American people, and internationally.

The bill of goods sold to them by Chalibi. The man so influenced by Israel, and Bush.

Now realizing the fraud of "Zionism", how the Holy Land is occupied by a false prophet, the profiteers of organized Crime. Private contractors, and corporations for total globalization starting with the wealth of the Middle East.

Take a close look at the last 60 years. A Conspiracy? Much more true then Democracy.

Turkey, Iran, Syria, Lybia, Lebanon, Egypt, Jordan and even Saudi's are waking up to the facts the Arab League of Nations face in the future. They all will have to fight for their rightful heritage.

The American people have already lost.

Since the election fraud of 2000, the American people have been in turmoil over the appointment.

An explanation should be in order.

Did the court appoint a President, Dictator, Reverend, Rabbi, or organized crime chief to preside at our White House? Or has the office become one and the same?

We have no questions on our minds that you appointed the "Underground Worlds" --God-Father" as vice president.

Is our government now exclusive to the Executive, Legislative, or Judicial Branch or have all three merged at the Oval office?

We realize that all of you receive large checks from our tax base, and from every lobby in this world. How-ever is there anyone working for the interest of America? It seems, do to the diligence of AIPAC, Israel is now the only beneficiary of such maneuvering, and the only real recipient of any effort by OUR government.

Such seems to be the consequences of another merger, the merger of Church & State. Of course such merger did not include moral values, ethics, or integrity. And is very evident it is the Axis of Evil.

Bush's Wiretaps: Impeachment not Immunity
Two years ago, the NY Times revealed George Bush has been illegally wiretapping our phones and emails for years. Bush publicly admitted signing the authorizations for illegal wiretaps over 30 times.
Bush's warrantless wiretaps are a flagrant violation of the Fourth Amendment. And under the 1978 FISA law, the penalty for each of Bush's illegal wiretaps is up to $10,000 and 5 years in prison. Bush may have wiretapped millions of Americans, so he should not only be impeached, but he should spend the rest of his life behind bars.

On Tuesday's Ed Schultz Show, Nancy Pelosi struggled to explain why she opposes impeaching Bush and Cheney. She said if anyone could prove Bush committed impeachable offenses, they should contact her.
Of course violating the Fourth Amendment and FISA is impeachable, and it's proved by Bush's confession (see above). Rewriting laws with signing statements is impeachable, and it's proved by the statements posted on the White House website and by a GAO study finding that in many cases Bush has proceeded to violate the laws he claims the right to violate. Refusing to comply with subpoenas is impeachable, and there is no dispute that Bush and Cheney have refused to comply.

The evidence collected at http://www.afterdowningstreet
Ten Reasons to Impeach George Bush and Dick Cheney
I ask Congress to impeach President Bush and Vice President Cheney for the following reasons:

1. Violating the United Nations Charter by launching an illegal "War of Aggression" against Iraq without cause, using fraud to sell the war to Congress and the public, misusing government funds to begin bombing without Congressional authorization, and subjecting our military personnel to unnecessary harm, debilitating injuries, and deaths.

2. Violating U.S. and international law by authorizing the torture of thousands of captives, resulting in dozens of deaths, and keeping prisoners hidden from the International Committee of the Red Cross.

3. Violating the Constitution by arbitrarily detaining Americans, legal residents, and non-Americans, without due process, without charge, and without access to counsel.

4. Violating the Geneva Conventions by targeting civilians, journalists, hospitals, and ambulances, and using illegal weapons, including white phosphorous, depleted uranium, and a new type of napalm.

5. Violating U.S. law and the Constitution through widespread wiretapping of the phone calls and emails of Americans without a warrant.

6. Violating the Constitution by using "signing statements" to defy hundreds of laws passed by Congress.

7. Violating U.S. and state law by obstructing honest elections in 2000, 2002, 2004, and 2006.

8. Violating U.S. law by using paid propaganda and disinformation, selectively and misleadingly leaking classified information, and exposing the identity of a covert CIA operative working on sensitive WMD proliferation for political retribution.

9. Subverting the Constitution and abusing Presidential power by asserting a "Unitary Executive Theory" giving unlimited powers to the President, by obstructing efforts by Congress and the Courts to review and restrict Presidential actions, and by promoting and

signing legislation negating the Bill of Rights and the Writ of Habeas Corpus.

10. Gross negligence in failing to assist New Orleans residents after Hurricane Katrina, in ignoring urgent warnings of an Al Qaeda attack prior to Sept. 11, 2001, and in increasing air pollution causing global warming.

By refusing to allow Saddam to flee with guarantees, Bush ensured that a land war would have to be fought. This is one of the greatest crimes any US president ever committed, and it is all the more contemptible for being rooted in mere pride and petulance.

He had a real offer in the hand, of Saddam's flight. He rejected it. By rejecting it, he will have killed at least a million persons and became one of the more monstrous figures in recent world history.

Now it is time for the American people to go to war against the FASCISM, of this our present form of government, that has assumed power over us..

The real problem with America is who is in the White House, a ventriloquist dummy who has spent 6 plus years being manipulated by Dick Cheney. Not only can NO progress be made on any issue until they are removed, unless they are impeached the amount of additional havoc they will wreck in the next 500 days is too terrible to contemplate.

In America those believing they are born to rule behave with such brutality to defend their rights, their property, their hold over society that they approach true fascism (This Administration..)

A COUP HAS OCCURRED!!

GOVERNMENT SOLD, NOT FOR SALE. FOREIGN POLICY IS ISRAEL & AIPAC CONTROLLED NO MATTER, WHO IS IN OFFICE.

OUR GOVERNMENT IS NOT FOR-SALE, IT HAS BEEN SOLD:

More then 150 million dollars have been raised from the American People, for the Democratic Party on lies to end the WAR.

This time it isn't the republicans telling the lies, it is all top 3 democrat candidates for the Democrat Party. Time after time, the deception has been, vote for me, and give me money I will immediately Leave IRAQ. The first thing to be done is BRING OUR TROOPS HOME. Not even redeploy. The claim was BRING THEM HOME.

Now after raising record amounts from individual Americans, we hear a different story. One that shows how special interest groups, foreign lobbies dictate to all parties. Republican, Democrat No longer matters.

Now to realize that the Fascist coupe, that has occurred, is a take over of both parties, Of both houses, now it does not matter. No one takes a second look at impeachment, or to hold ANYONE accountable.

It is a sad state of affairs. America no longer has a real choice. We vote only as an impudent citizen.
Our choice is based on, vote for a female, vote for a black, vote for a conservative, vote for a liberal, Vote for an actor, but the REAL ISSUES for AMERICA are off the TABLE,

IMPEACHMENT, WAR, HEALTH CARE, IMMIGRATION, BORDER CONTROL, OUT-SOURCING, FOREIGN TRADE, REAL CAMPAIGN REFORM, CHECKS & BALANCE, CENSORSHIP, CONSTITUTIONAL VIOLATIONS, PRIVATE ARMIES, HUMAN RIGHTS, LOBBIES, EVERY ISSUE SEEMS TO BE A VIOLATION OF

SOME HATE CRIME. ALL MOSTLY CALLED, ANTI-SEMENTIC. NOW WE FACE A GLOBAL ANTI-SEMENTIC LAW. LOBBIED AND PAID FOR BY ISRAEL & AIPAC.

Talk about Arrogance! Bush signs a law judging the rest of the world. While Bush ignores the ruling of the UN and the World Court! It's not even a good law! That's why the world needs a bipartisan world rather than one superpower. The power goes into their head!

The world does not exist for Jews and Israel only, but all of our policies and new laws, and most decisions are now made with their interest in mind only. WHY IS THAT!!!

Americans need to revolt. We are losing all.

Read: President Jimmy Carter's book. Read: Professor's John Mearsheimer & Steven Walt. Read: Richard Clark's book. Read & Listen: To weapons inspector Scott Ritter.

How about a panel of these individuals, not Media personalities, or other special interest personalities, let them voice what is going on, what needs to be done, And most important what candidate, OR candidates they would endorse IF ANY. The changes that need to be made IMMEDIATELY.

That is because two things come together that with the acceptance for various reasons of the Congress – Democrats and Republicans – and the public and the media, we have freed the White House – the president and the vice president – from virtually any restraint by Congress, courts, media, public, whatever.

And on the other hand, the people who have this unrestrained power are crazy."

'A Coup Has Occurred'

Bush and Cheney have been subverting our Constitution since they took office. They've also been undermining the basic principles on which America was founded, the principles of liberty, equality and justice for all. They've corrupted Congress, taken over the mainstream media to use as their propaganda organ, used the military to further their private interests, drained the treasury, hastened environmental catastrophe, and terrorized the population with rumors of false flag operations, bird flu epidemics, concentration camps meant for us, etc, etc, etc. Cheney has issued veiled hints about nuking an American city- the internet is buzzing with concern about the missing nuclear-tipped cruise missile.

It's now clear that from the start, the goal of Bush and Cheney has been to create the conditions necessary to institute a dictatorship.

CONRESS: THE BUSH/CHENEY & ISRAELI CRONIES, LET THEM GET AWAY WITH IT.

TURKEYS WITH THEIR HEADS IN THE SAND.

TURKEY IS A STAUNCH ALLY OF ISRAEL AND THE USA. IGNORING THE ATROCITIES OF WAR, AND HUMAN RIGHTS VIOLATIONS ON IT'S NEIGHBORS.
NO OBJECTION TO THE ABUSES OF LEBANON, THE KILLING OF OVER A MILLION IRAQI'S. BUT WATCH TURKEY WILL BE THE NEXT TARGET AFTER SYRIA AND IRAN. TURKEY IS IGNORANT TO THE FACT OF HOW THEY ARE PRESENTLY BEING USED BY THE REAL AXIS OF EVIL. ZIONIST TAKE OVER..

ONLY BEING USED FOR FLY ZONES, AND SUPPLY LINES, NEXT, MILITARY BASES FOR ISRAEL & USA.

Subject: FW: BRING THE TROOPS HOME (WE ARE DOWN RIGHT ASHAMED, NOT EMBARASSED, BY THIS OUR GOVERNMENT, TOP--DOWN)

Subject: BRING THE TROOPS HOME

THE TRUTH PREVAILS:

BLACKWATER SECURITY AND OTHERS:

For weeks, months, years, it has been know by many Americans, that Iraqi civilians were being indiscriminately killed.

Enough evidence has been established, that such now is becoming brought out from Secrecy, and from under the cover-up.

The question now becomes direct to Military Commanders & the Pentagon. The Iraqis, the contractors, military personnel have been witness to these kinds of abuses for the entire time we have occupied Iraq. It certainly does not seem to the rest of us, that that would be part of the LIBERATION. You will have a hard time convincing anyone, that part of the responsibility toward accountability for these criminal acts, does not fall directly on very top Military & civilian leadership.

Unlike Viet Nam, where the blame was pushed down to a Lt. Cali, the top shall be held to blame.

The death toll on Iraqi civilians speaks for itself. Impossible, to have been missed by top leadership.

"THUGS" EQUIPPED BETTER THAN THE TROOPS, ON YOUR TAX DOLLARS..
WHILE OUR TROOPS DIE !!

What little news we have gotten on the Private Security company Blackwater.

Did anyone notice how well equipped they are in comparison to our troops? Folks that was done on your taxes FOR Private corporations. WOW!!

I really don't see how that is supporting our troops,all this rhetoric on how the republicans support our troops. The reality is the money has gone to provide Security on the oil wells, Permanent construction of bases, and on an Embassy, largest in the world. Just why is that?

WHERE HAS CONGRESS AND THE MEDIA BEEN. IN SOMEONES POCKET!!

MR. PRESIDENT AND VICE PRESIDENT, SOMEONE HAS "BETRAYED—US"!!

MORE UNJUSTIFABLE WAR CRIMES!!

A British polling agency has determined that more than one million Iraqi citizens have died as a result of the Iraq war. This report follows survey results released last fall by Lancet, the prestigious medical magazine which gave a conservative estimate of 650,000 deaths. Opinion Research Business found that the death rate in Iraq increased by 1.2 million people since the U.S.-led invasion began .

Due to the current crisis, approximately 2,000 Iraqis are forced to flee their homes every day. More than 2.2 million Iraqis have already fled to neighboring countries such as Syria and Jordan, where they face a daily struggle to survive. Jordan has closed its borders, and Syria plans to next month. Soon, Iraqis threatened with death will literally have no way to flee.

The atrocities are just coming to light in Congress, but have been in sight for 4 years by many..

The government has silenced media that wasn't

already in their pocket. Or again was that Blackwater doing the administrations dirty work.

But of course they get immunity!! 128 Journalist have been killed in Iraq.

INVESTIGATE, INTERVIEW, AND INVESTIGATE INTERVIEW. NOT JUST OUR TROOPS, BUT ALL THE COALITION TROOPS THAT HAVE PULLED OUT...

Amazing how when you stop killing. The completely WAR pace slows down!!

WILL WE GET TRUTHFUL REPORTS NOW ??

Blackwater USA is an out-of-control outfit indifferent to Iraqi civilian casualties, according to a picture painted in a critical report released by a key congressional committee. Blackwater has had to fire 122 people over the past three years for problems ranging from misusing weapons, alcohol and drug violations, inappropriate conduct, and violent behavior,

BUSH CONNECTION: The connections include the firm's chief operating officer Joseph Schmitz, who was tapped by President Bush in 2002 to "oversee and police the Pentagon's military contracts as the Defense Department's Inspector General."

Blackwater has received more than $832 million in contracts from the State Department. (Almost $4 billion has been spent on security contracts since the U.S. invasion of Iraq in 2003, Waxman's committee estimates.)

Bush administration and Republican party, including:
• Erik Prince, Blackwater's founder, who has donated "roughly $300,000 to Republican candidates and political action committees. Through his Freiheit Foundation, he also gave $500,000 to Prison Fellowship Ministries, run by former Nixon official Charles Colson, in 2000."
• J. Cofer Black, Blackwater Vice Chairman, a 28-year veteran of the CIA Van Heuvelen describes as "one of the more prominent faces associated with the Bush administration's interrogation and extraordinary rendition policies." Black is also a senior adviser to GOP presidential candidate Mitt Romney.
• Rob Richer, Vice President for Intelligence, who is the former head of the CIA Near East Division. "In 2003," according to Salon "he briefed President Bush on the nascent Iraqi insurgency. In late 2004, he became the associate deputy director in the CIA's Directorate of Operations, making him the second-ranking official for clandestine operations."
• Fred Fielding, a former outside counsel for the firm, who "has had a long career as a lawyer to prominent Republicans. From 1970 to 1972, he was an associate White House counsel in the Nixon administration; from 1972 to 1974, he was present for the denouement of that administration as deputy White House counsel." Fielding is a former counsel to President Reagan and current White House counsel to President Bush.

• Ken Starr, another counsel to Blackwater, who was hired by the firm in 2006, is best known "as the Independent Counsel who investigated Bill Clinton. He revealed the intimate details of Clinton's affair with intern Monica Lewinsky in the infamous Starr Report and set in motion Clinton's impeachment by Congress.

State has done little to reign in or punish rogue contractors.

There is no evidence in the documents that the committee has reviewed that the State Department sought to restrain Blackwater's actions, raised concerns about the number of shooting incidents involving Blackwater or the company's high rate of shooting first, or detained Blackwater contractors for investigation, The private security firm Blackwater USA, has numerous links to the White House as well as many current and former Republicans.

The corruption, and atrocities will not stop until we pull our troops home, and Impeach this administration....

Subject: MORE AND MORE CENSORSHIP !!

This is Very dangerous. It appears that Sara Roy is the most recent example of silencing.

It seems that the ruling elite and compliant media do not want criticism of, or any rational examination of the policies of Israel and will do what it can to silence any dissenting views.

It is obvious that the militarists and right wing benefit from the concept of the Muslim world as our "enemy" and for this reason don't want the American people to reconsider our unquestioning support of Israel. Yet, especially when the Israeli government is publically calling for an attack on Iran, this is exactly the time when our relationship with Israel needs to be examined.

I don't know if we can do anything concrete about Sara Roy's silencing, but we must be aware of and fight against the silencing of a dissenting view of Israel, an examination of its treatment of the Palestinians and Israel's critical role in determining our foreign policy-- AH]

BOOK REVIEW

Hamas: Politics, Charity and Terrorism in the Service of Jihad by Matthew Levitt. Yale University Press, in cooperation with the Washington Institute for Near East Policy, 2006.

Sara Roy
Center for Middle Eastern Studies, Harvard University
http://mepc.org/journal_vol14/0707_roy.asp

Author's Note:
This review, published here in its entirety, was originally commissioned by The Fletcher Forum of World Affairs, the official foreign-policy journal at the Fletcher School at Tufts University.

Between the time I was invited to write the review and the time I was told it would be published, over two months had passed during which I had had several exchanges, some of them difficult, with the editorial staff. However, by the end of the process the editor-in-chief, with whom I had been working, was pleased with the review, and so was I. He sent me an e-PDF of the review as it would appear in the journal (Volume 31:1 Winter 2007). The PDF version of the page proofs revealed that the editor had excerpted two relevant sentences (featured in sidebars) to highlight observations that I had offered in the review:

1. "While there can be no doubt that, since its inception, Hamas has engaged in violence and armed struggle, and has been the primary force behind the horrific suicide bombings inside Israel, Levitt's presentation reduces this increasingly complex and sophisticated

organization to an insular, one-dimensional...entity dedicated solely to violence...and Israel's destruction."

2. "The ability of Hamas to reinterpret itself over time through processes of radicalization, de-radicalization, de-militarization, and re-radicalization is a pronounced and common theme in its historical evolution." During a subsequent exchange the editor-in-chief wrote, "Thank you for your hard work as well. It's a good review." I believed that was the end of the matter. Just a few days later, I received the following e-mail message from the same editor-in-chief:

Dear Ms. Roy:

...After careful review and much consideration of the merits of your piece, we have decided that we are ultimately unable to publish your review for this edition. Your review was evaluated by several of our editors and an external editor for objectivity. Unfortunately, they disagreed with my decision to publish your review for the following reasons: despite their agreement with many of your points, all reviewers found the piece one-sided. This one-sidedness dissuaded readers from reading the piece to the end; ultimately, this last point is the most important. Although I found your arguments valuable, if readers consistently feel this way, I am unable to move forward with a piece. My apologies for the way in which this process was carried out, and for the time that you spent on editing the piece. Thank you once again for your submission and your efforts. If you would like to discuss this further, please feel free to e-mail me.

In more than 20 years of writing and publishing I have never experienced such behavior or encountered what to me, at least, is so blatant a case of censorship. I am therefore extremely grateful to Anne Joyce and Stephen Magro for agreeing to publish the review in Middle East Policy.

MORE AND MORE: EDITING HAS BECOME CENSORSHIP!!!
Subject: STAFFERS ON THE HILL

Georgetown University--George Washington University, private Universities.

Harvard University--Yale University, private Universities.

All above Universities are highly influenced by AIPAC LOBBY. To the point that administrations, professors, and contributions come from AIPAC and other organizations with ISRAELI influence on such education system.

To the extreme point that our Congressmen & Senators are unduly influenced by their staffers that come from those universities, also taking their advisor members from the professors of such universities.

We also feel that the SCREENING of information, e-mails, documents, even editorials, are scanned by staffers to present only information benificial to the AIPAC, ISRAELI cause. That BILLS introduced on the floor, are even written by such staffers. That PORK entered into or attached to BILLS are done so by staffers.

When we the AMERICAN people request reform of GOVERNMENT such practice should also be reformed. It seems our elected officials are immediately guided into this corrupt system.

Enough interviews have been done with past officials etc, that points this out.

BUT year after year, the system of undo influence continues. EVEN to the point that all trips to Israel for INFORMATION GATHERING, is done to take away any support for the true victims of conflict in the Middle East. The Palestenian people, Iraq, Syria, Lebanon, Iraq, Jordan, Egypt, and soon to be Iran, if their influence continues.

The Church organizations in this country bought into this Israeli propaganda along time ago. Seemingly, and wrongfully agreeing with the human rights violations, abuses and genocide for the last 60 years.

It is time our complete system of governing, foreign policy, and foreign influences be REFORMED.

Do not "underestimate" the "anger," "frustration," and "determination," of your citizens who demand "justice and fairness."
Next: Do not underestimate the influence of such "RELIGIOUS" institution on State & Local governments, and most all other educational institutions, even down to the level of high schools. Investigate AIPAC and such organizations activities completely. OUR constitution is ignored when it comes to separation of Church, including synagogues, we demand reform, And FAIR taxation on all.

Subject: PHONE COMPANIES MONEY WILL NOW BUY CONGRESS!!

Phone companies money will count more, then will the law, and ethics. To think we vote for them, we pay them, we expect some kind of oversight and hold criminals accountable, but we will witness Business as usual. Acountability, like Impeachment, is off the table, any type check & balance is off the table. We know the only checks that are on the table, check after check.

Newsweek recently reported that the nation's biggest phone companies, "working closely with the White House, have mounted a secretive lobbying campaign to get Congress to quickly approve a measure wiping out all private lawsuits against them" for helping the Bush administration illegally wiretap innocent Americans.1
Yesterday, President Bush weighed in publicly, promising to veto an upcoming bill dealing with our nation's wiretapping policy if it doesn't give corporations retroactive immunity for their lawbreaking. Pending lawsuits could be the only way Americans ever find out

how far Bush went in breaking the law—Bush's threat yesterday is an attempted cover-up.

Some Democrats like Sen. Russ Feingold immediately said no to Bush. But House Majority Leader Steny Hoyer said retroactive immunity "is not off the table."

It dam well should be off the table. Is everyone being black mailed like dear little Nancy??

The 110Th congress has become worst than the 109Th, Did you think that would be possible with the promises of 2006??

Before you give immunity, think how many of those tapped ended up a blackwater target. Or some other agency target. Or locked up with the key thrown away, because they oppose the present policies. Think beyond, we know it is being done, and it will not be covered up. Even though you all Try to cover up. How many journalists have been murdered, why?? How?? Where??

Subject: TAX AND SPEND BULL-CRAP!!

As citizens of the USA, we keep hearing about the TAX and SPEND Democrats.

The National debt of $9,010,980,950 was created PRIOR to Democrats having any power over the RUBBER STAMPING of bad policy from the REPUBLICANS. Deficits higher Then any time in History. TAX CUTS to the very rich. With 69% of the corporations in this country, not paying ANY tax at all.

A WAR, that is a WAR for profit by these same politicians and corporations, that authorized all the spending by the BUSH administration. The REPUBLICANS created a debt to a communist country, CHINA; for most all of this debt.

PLEASE, explain to us, the AMERICAN people, just how all this money will Be paid. How will we ever get to our own domestic problems and infrastructure,

If TAXES, particularly on Rich and corporations that got us into this dam mess, are not raised.

We realize that the REPUBLICANS, plan to pass it all on to our children, and their children for generation after generation.

We the AMERICAN people want some spending to stop. IRAQ war, Foreign aid to ISRAEL, and corrupt profits from WAR.

We feel that the foreign lobby should be taxed. We also feel, that the tax free Properties of Churches should now be TAXED.

Up until, the Court appointment of 2000, for president. We enjoyed the policy of separation of Church & State. They have enjoyed the privilege of NO TAX.

HOW_EVER, they preached from the pulpit for war support. Churches and Particularly Rabbi's in the synagogues. That the IRS has refused to look at, in violation of our constitution.

WHAT WE CONSIDER MORE THEN FAIR WITH ALL THE INVOLVEMENT IN OUR GOVERNMENT.

SHALL NOW PAY THEIR SHARE.

William H. Rehnquist spoke for the court:
Both tax exemptions and tax deductibility are a form of subsidy that is administered through the tax system. A tax exemption has much the same effect as a cash grant to the organization of the amount of tax it would have to pay on its income.

The significance of this decision is often overlooked. If tax exemption is a form of subsidy, then church property tax exemption is a clear violation of the establishment clause of the First Amendment. All that is necessary to make church property tax exemption a thing of the past is for an irate taxpayer who is tired of high taxes to file suit to force churches to pay their "fair share."

Tenth Circuit Court addressed, and held that "tax exemption is a privilege, a matter of grace rather than a right."

The question of tax exemption for churches is clear: the foundation has been laid for taxing church property and perhaps even church income.

As the budget deficits of the federal, state and local governments increase, the possibility of taxing church property also rises -- despite the long history of tax exemption.

We are sick and tired of the "Zionist-Movement" the cost of the "WAR" they demanded, the amount of holdings & investments rather then any amount of return to the community. The threat of Falwell to use 200,000 preachers to preach his message from the pulpit is not only wrong it is unlimited use of propaganda!

The millions spent on foolish campaigns designed to shape or change public opinion in regard to this or that: divorce, birth control, the falseness of the Darwinian theory, or almost anything in connection with science and history! The blather about saints and cures and bringing all to Jesus, the while taxes are evaded and the scummy politicians whom they endorse, or even nominate and elect to office, proceed to rob the public in favor of the corporations and churches whom they serve! No wonder ignorance, no wonder illusion, when those with power in the religious field knowingly delude and mislead the masses! The things told them! That it is important to vote for this or that crook; uphold religion; it is good for the people to go to war, to put religion in the schools, to give into the hands of these mental bandits the care and education of all children, so that they may be properly enslaved by religion! (A slave, in my opinion, is the man who does not think for himself. A man with knowledge is not powerless.) But always with suave and polished words.

How about a Robertson or Bush Whisper! God has told me, and I will tell you, and you shall follow and sustain me as my servant who am the servant of God! SURE!

One would think from that that the Churches were a branch of the Government, a public institution, whereas they are only semipublic, being under the control of a special group of patrons, and as such should be taxed and made to pay the same as any other self-aggrandizing corporation.

The State now should not permit them to go tax free, and should, should it not? enjoy and participate in any money-making of this nature, which is certainly no legitimate function of religion. Then look close at the MONEY!!

Well now, church buildings alone in America, without parsonages, investments, securities, schools, orphanages, hospitals and monasteries, are valued in the trillions. Investments such as in Defense etc, also will be in the trillions. Do they ever cough up in crisis,

No they just manage the money from the congregation they solicit it from. Lets call it Alms instead of Tyethings. America now represented by the money-mad leaders who are dictating not only the economics but the philosophy of the country and using the religionists to help them. Or might it be the fool led by fools.

We will sue for tax fairness due to the last six years of Church involvement in Politics, openly judging people with a different political view, telling a congregation they must support the republican party, and support an unjust "WAR".

Now pay for it, I left the Church because I'm proud to be a Democrat, American, a Christian, but no longer a member of any denomination that supports corruption and/or WAR. BLAME THE PAT ROBERTSONS AND JERRY FALWELLS FOR INVOLVING CHURCH & STATE.

I pay Taxes for your injustice, now you will also.

I REQUEST THE ACLU TO TAKE UP SUCH ISSUE FOR THE BENEFIT OF ALL THOSE PAYING SUCH COST !!

Subject: THE TRUE, AND ONLY HERO'S OF 911, FIREFIGHTERS, AND POLICEMEN. NO NOT ONE POLITICIAN, IS ANY TYPE OF HERO IN ANYONE'S EYES.

THE COUNTRY'S LEADERS HAVE All but forgot the true hero's of 911.

People who gave life & limb in attempt to save those lost. Trained to aid & assist life, not see it taken.

Now they stand alone, observing the incomplete investigations, the incomplete truth, and the political rhetoric of that fateful day.

The firefighters and policemen, America's heroes, wonder why so much secrecy. Why so many discrepancies of the facts. Now with all the suffering by members that responded, that now faces disability or death, because of the hazardous materials, injuries, & trauma . Do not get help or answers.

The death toll of that day, the losses to all families of 911, used as political rhetoric, and a tool for unjustified WAR.

Osama Bin Laden, the accused perpetrator, still on the run, while our government engages in a civil War in Iraq.

So much more death & destruction, 3950 troops killed, 1 million civilians killed, 28000 troops injured, thousands of Iraqi's injured, 2 million displaced.

America's heroes are in support of the troops and their families, they want accountability for all that has transpired prior to, and since 911. The truth is demanded, accountability is demanded..

It is time for the American People to hire private investigative firms, dig out the truth, we shall use that same techniques this false flag government uses, private military that does not answer to Congress or the pentagon.

Well, we guess true information is forthcoming to America also.

Join in now,
Subject: AMERICA: WE DO NOT HAVE ANYONE REPRESENTING US IN THIS GOVERNMENT. "TOTAL FACISM BY ZIONIST" NO MORE DEMACRACY BY AND FOR THE PEOPLE !!

WE NOW CAN CLEARLY SEE IT!! THE COALITION, BUSH & HIS CRONIES HAVE FOR THE IRAQ WAR, AND THE CONTINUATION OF SUCH ATROCITIES ARE NONE OTHER THEN THE "110TH CONGRESS". NO REAL ATTEMPTS TO END SUCH. JUST RETHORIC, BUT VOTE ALONG AGAIN AND AGAIN..

SOMEONE SURE "BETRAYED--US"   (THE   110TH CONGRESS)

"THUGS" EQUIPPED BETTER THAN THE TROOPS, ON YOUR TAX DOLLARS.. WHILE OUR TROOPS DIE !!
 What little news we have gotten on the Private Security company Blackwater.

Did anyone notice how well equipped they are in comparison to our troops? Folks that was done on your taxes FOR Private corporations. WOW!!

I really don't see how that is supporting our troops,all this rhetoric on how the republicans support our troops. The reality is the money has gone to provide Security on the oil wells, Permanent construction of bases, and on an Embassy, largest in the world. Just why is that?

How can they claim support for our troops??

WHERE HAS CONGRESS AND THE MEDIA BEEN. IN SOMEONES POCKET!!

MR. PRESIDENT AND VICE PRESIDENT, SOMEONE HAS "BETRAYED—US"!!

MORE UNJUSTIFABLE WAR CRIMES!!

How many died from the "Friendly Fire of Blackwater"?

A British polling agency has determined that more than one million Iraqi citizens have died as a result of the Iraq war. This report follows survey results released last fall by Lancet, the prestigious medical magazine which gave a conservative estimate of 650,000 deaths. Opinion Research Business found that the death rate in Iraq increased by 1.2 million people since the U.S.-led invasion began in 2003.

If our troops killed 45,000 as Bush claims, who killed the rest, "Blackwater"??

Due to the current crisis, approximately 2,000 Iraqis are forced to flee their homes every day. More than 2.2 million Iraqis have already fled to neighboring countries such as Syria and Jordan, where they face a daily struggle to survive. Jordan has closed its borders, and Syria plans to next month. Soon, Iraqis threatened with death will literally have no way to flee.

The atrocities are just coming to light in Congress, but have been in sight for 4 years by many..

The government has silenced media that wasn't already in their pocket. Or again was that Blackwater doing the administrations dirty work. But of course they get immunity!! 128 Journalist have been killed in Iraq.

INVESTIGATE, INTERVIEW, INVESTIGATE INTERVIEW. NOT JUST OUR TROOPS, BUT ALL THE COALITION TROOPS THAT HAVE PULLED OUT...

"IMPEACH BUSH/CHENEY--NOW !!

" A preacher of the gospel ought not to be patiently listened to those, who eloquently promotes the blessings of liberty or occupation by WAR ,as if they make them free, while in fact hold their fellow-humans, administer torture, death and distruction. Take their property and resources in a most dreadful and lacerating bondage." Might that be the precise reasoning for separation of Church & State?

 NOW IMPEACH, AND HOLD THOSE ACCOUNTABLE FOR THEIR CRIMES AND HYPOCRACY !!

 QUESTIONS TO HAVE ANSWERED!!

PLEASE:

Go back to 2004. What were the statements made by president Bush and the republicans, about Civil War in Iraq, and what our options would be if that happened. I remember ALL the claims by them prior to the elections. IF it were to develop into a civil WAR. We would protect our troops, and with-draw them from Iraq.

That was stated by Bush/Cheney, Rice, Rumsfelt, and all their cronies. NOW OUR TROOPS DIE IN THE MIDDLE OF A CIVIL WAR, and we stay the course of failure.

QUESTIONS; ATROCITIES, CENSORSHIP, MONITORING, FOREIGN LOBBY, AND GOVERNMENT FOR SALE..

 IT AMOUNTS TO ORGANIZED CRIME:

Interview returning troops, regarding atrocities by Blackwater under immunity in Iraq.

 The government has just made congress.org change their web page. Messages that were posted have been censored off. Capitol Advantage.

 We do not have freedom of press. The following posted Wed. has been removed , censored.

 MR. PRESIDENT, WE THE PEOPLE HAVE QUESTIONS! LET THE TRUTH HURT WHERE IT SHOULD, DC!!

 Mr. President:

You call this War of yours a coalition. You tell about all the international support you have for the atrocities committed on the Iraqi people.

We see that we the USA have 160,000 TROOPS presently in Iraq.130,000 prior to the surge.Next summer we may be back to that number.

We ask how many of the surge troops total are from any other country? It seems while we surge. All other support withdraws, which nothing has been stated about that.

We see UK has had 5,500 troops there, and are pulling out. Next may have 2,500 etc.

It now has cost us a total of ONE trillion dollars most of which has been profit for corruption such as Halliburton & Black water.

How much has this coalition of other countries put up for such cost?

We have lost 3,790 troops. How many lives have been lost by other countries? We have had 26,000 troops with major injuries, what about others??

We also know the involvement to go to war was for the benefit of Israel. How much money have they lost' how many lives?

We also know you ignore the resolutions by the UN against Israel and atrocities committed against the Palestinian people. Do you realize the effect of such of the entire middle east?.

Sir, how can you call this a coalition? When in fact this is a Bush / Cheney war, a war for corporate profit, a coalition of cronies.

Now, we know you will refer everything to 911 and al-qaeda. BUT we also see many discrepancies in that. Questions we know will never be answered to the American people.

We believe you should leave office. Many prosecutions should occur with-in your administration for WAR crimes.

We also realize that these are questions not being ask by Other officials, simply because of their own involvement With special interest lobbies, corporate and Foreign.

What we as the American people see out of all this, is how Much reform we need in government.

We want our troops redeployed home to protect our borders.

We do not feel safer at all. We fear your form of government, such is becoming Fascism.

The hatred you brought against America. Al-Qaeda did not exist in Iraq prior. It was in Afghanistan. Now all over the world.

Grown drastically since the beginning of WAR on terror.

Will you really tell us again, that you're heavenly FATHER Told you to do all this??

Let the TRUE facts hurt where they should hurt, and that is all in Washington, DC.

Call the coalition what it actually is, a coalition of NEOCONS, ZIONIST only.

Newly leaked Pentagon documents have confirmed the military has been monitoring and collecting intelligence on anti-war groups across the country. Peace protests are being described as threats and the military is collecting data on who is attending demonstrations. We speak with William Arkin, the former Army intelligence officer, who obtained the secret Pentagon documents.

For those who didn't hear it already, two of the seven young soldiers on active duty in Iraq who wrote the extraordinarily powerful op-ed in the New York Times condemning the Bush administration strategy and propaganda claims of "success" in the war, were killed in Iraq earlier this week.

Every retiring general in recent years has criticized the war in Iraq AFTER leaving the military. Where are the active duty generals to match the courage of their lower ranking colleagues?

BLACKWATER HAS COMPLETE IMMUNITY--EVEN WHEN, ASSASSIGNATING JOURNALIST.

128 NOW KILLED IN IRAQ. DO WE GET THE NEWS??

THE INSIDE HISTORY OF THE ISRAEL LOBBY

Former top CIA analysts Kathleen and Bill Christison give CounterPunchers the real scoop on the Israel lobby and precisely how powerful it is. Read how US presidents from Wilson, through FDR to Truman were manipulated by the Zionist lobby; how Israel bent LBJ, Reagan and Clinton to its purpose; how Bush's White House has been the West Wing of the Israeli government; how Washington's revolving doors send full-time Israel lobbyists from think-tanks to the National Security Council and the Pentagon's Office of Special Plans.

An unregistered Foreign Lobby, has purchased the "Government for Sale" including the Clintons and Rudy Giuliani. PLEASE we need new direction.

Obama and Edwards for 2008.

Subject: WHO DO YOU SELF-RIGHTEOUS POLITICIANS (ZIONIST) THINK YOU ARE KIDDING.

PULL-OUT IS THE ONLY WIN

AMERICA AND THE AMERICAN PEOPLE ARE BLEEDING TO THE POINT OF HEMORRAGE:

The corruption of, and the "WAR FOR PROFIT", Led by the republican--Israeli organized crime syndicate has brought this country to the point of bankruptcy. Led by, but with the purchase of several Polarized individuals, from both sides of the isle.

Not only bankrupt financially, but moral values, ethics, and all domestic issues.

We were promised border control, health coverage, Good employment opportunities etc. etc. NOT one domestic issue has been fulfilled.

There is great concern over the 911 facts, and what is the "TRUTH". Thus brings up a question about What the real facts are, in the relationship with Osama Bin Laden, Bush administration, and the Royal family, of Saudi Arabia. The money behind Al Quida. The new weapons agreement brings up some real issues, does it not?

It's all a lie. All of it. The IEDs from Iran is a lie. The suggestions that we might have some cosmetic troop withdrawals is a lie. It's a lulling tactic by the most malevolent constitutional frauds yet. They have no intention of EVER withdrawing, redeploying or anything else remotely like that. They're determined to carpet bomb Iran instead. And then we'll be REALLY stuck, at perpetual world war with a billion Muslims who mostly just wanted to be left alone. How convenient, Bin Laden comes up with a tape, every time Bush/ Cheney needs it, did they ever go after him like they did Sadam. ?? Some question if we should look in Crawford, Texas.

82 % of the American people want the Troops home. Also want impeachment of this entire administration, and want the WAR CRIMINALS prosecuted including Gonzales.

We liberated Iraq, now let them settle their own civil war. It is their wealth, let them rebuild on it themselves. We have spent all possible, for the benefit of Israel & the Profiteers.

Now it is time for the American people to go to war against the FASCISM, of this our present form of government, that has assumed power over us..

The real problem with America is who is in the White House, a ventriloquist dummy who has spent 6 plus years being manipulated by Dick Cheney. Not only can NO progress be made on any issue until they are removed, unless they are impeached the amount of additional havoc they will wreck in the next 500 days is too terrible to contemplate.

In America those believing they are born to rule behave with such brutality to defend their rights, their property, their hold over society that they approach true fascism (This Administration..)

This week Bush made it worse by authorizing by executive order the start of an invasion of unregulated, unsafe Mexican trucks. This was after the House voted 411-3 in May to forbid this, but then the Senate again got suckered by the White House into not acting on the Safe American Roads Act of 2007 before the recess.

Congress has turned itself into a very bad, cowardly joke, and only acting on impeachment can redeem them.

The outsourcing of even the jobs of Americans LIVING in this country is just a blip on the radar compared with the increasingly loud drum beats that Cheney is absolutely bent on a massive, blitz style attack on Iran, while all "too dumb to be president" can do is muse about how much money he will make on the lecture circuit after he leaves office. The only public speaking we need to hear from those two is their testimony at their war crimes trial, which such a premeditated attack on Iran would cry out for, the SAME Iran who offered to HELP us stop Al Qaida immediately after 9/11. Why didn't Bush/Cheney Want help, will we ever know who was who on the 911 pre-war plans.??

Only impeachment can save us. Only your activism with the simple act of engaging your friends and neighbors to speak out can save us. You have cast your own vote. We are asking you to do more. We all have to do more. It's going to be a footrace between impeachment and the planned Iran attack. We have enough time to stop them.

The American economy is not a goat to be sacrificed. Our brave men and women in our armed forces are not goats to be sacrificed. All Cheney and Bush are doing is trying to stall dealing with reality in Iraq, to try to saddle the next president with their monumental debacle. Bush was quoted saying exactly that in his new biography, that his PLAN is to PLAY for time until winter, while America continues to bleed to death in a hopeless geopolitical quagmire, abandoned now by even our last hardcore ally, the British.

Impeaching Bush WITHOUT going after Cheney first (or at the same time) would be like firing Charley McCarthy without canning Edgar Bergen. And we need you help in this initiative. Join us in helping to mobilize the voices to make impeachment a reality.

"US interference in Iraq" has not help the country move forward. We all know its time to leave. Military leaders seem to support stay the course, like some magic will happen.

Magic will only happen when we leave, and with-draw support for Israel's genocide of its neighbors.

From their killing of our President Kennedy, to 911, to Iraq, and now attempt on Iran & Syria to create even more war for the USA to take care of.
NO LONGER, YOU CREATED IT YOU TAKE CARE OF IT.

We American people will and are "Cutting and Running" from the real problem of the Middle East. ISRAEL!!

AMERICANS HAVE SPOKE, " CUT AND RUN" FROM AIPAC, WINEP, MOSSAD, AND ISRAEL: ENOUGH IS ENOUGH, RESPECT THE RESOLUTIONS AGAINST ISRAEL:

By now many Americans are aware that Israel, with a population of only 5.8 million people, is the largest recipient of U.S. foreign aid, and that Israel's aid plus U.S. aid to Egypt's 65 million people for keeping the peace with Israel has, for many years, consumed more than half of the U.S. bi-lateral foreign aid budget world-wide.

Besides its financial cost, unwavering U.S. support for Israel, exacts a huge price in American prestige and credibility overseas. Further, Israel's powerful U.S. lobby has been a major factor in delaying campaign finance reform, and also in the removal from American political life of some of our most distinguished public servants, members of Congress and even presidents.

Americans seem constantly astounded at our foreign policy failures in the Middle East. This stems from a ignorance of the background of the Israeli-Palestinian dispute, which in turn results from a reluctance by the mainstream U.S. media to present these facts objectively.

Even our European and Asian allies have joined in deploring the perpetual American tilt toward Israel. Yet Americans seem oblivious to such examples of how their Israel-centered Middle East policies are isolating the US in the world.

Claims that there are positive aspects of the U.S.-Israeli relationship seldom stand up to scrutiny.

Never before have we pre-empted a war. Now close to 700,000 Iraq's have been killed.(civilian Iraqi's) and there is no exit plan then, now or for the near future. We feel it is time for accountability.
IMPEACH AND PROSECUTE---BRING BACK THE LAWYERS THAT WERE READY TO DO SO PRIOR TO THEIR BEING FIRED..............

NO MORE WAR. PLEASE READ AND TAKE ACTION NOW!!

CALL YOUR SENATORS RIGHT NOW AND DEMAND THEY VOTE DOWN THE LIEBERMAN-KYL AMENDMENT

In case you thought it was just an aberrant moment of lunacy last week when Lieberman pressed General Petraeus for an attack on Iran, just before the weekend he introduced an amendment to the defense bill to authorize exactly that.

No, we are not kidding. He has drafted language that any impartial observer would interpret as a DECLARATION OF WAR against Iran, and he is pressing for a vote as fast as possible.

ACTION PAGE:
http://www.usalone.com/no_iran_war_declaration.php

Here is the language from the amendment:

(3) that it should be the policy of the United States to combat, contain, and roll back the violent activities and destabilizing influence inside Iraq of the Government of the Islamic Republic of Iran, its foreign facilitators such as Lebanese Hezbollah, and its indigenous Iraqi proxies;

(4) to support the prudent and calibrated use of all instruments of United States national power in Iraq, including diplomatic, economic, intelligence, and military instruments, in support of the policy described in paragraph (3) with respect to the Government of the Islamic Republic of Iran and its proxies.

The policy of the U.S should be to "combat" Iran with "all" "military instruments"?!? You can be absolutely certain that those are the ONLY words Dick Cheney and George Bush will see or care about.

ACTION PAGE:
http://www.usalone.com/no_iran_war_declaration.php

We need every warm body we can muster to call and email their senators RIGHT NOW, before they pull another fast one and sneak this one through in the dead of the night. Call them toll free at 800 828-0498, 800 614 2803 or 866 340 9281, and the submit the action form below to make sure your message gets through.

Just yesterday, Newsweek reported that Cheney had recently made overtures to Israel to get them to launch an attack against Iran, to try to provoke an all out conflagration. It seems every day there is a new story leaked about their aggressive preparations for The Debacle, Part 2. And just as in the lead up to the Iraq invasion, they will keep lying, lying and lie some more about their intentions until they've shot off every cruise missile in the military inventory.

We need your voice, and the voices of everyone else you know, and we them now. We need to absolutely flood the Capitol with phone calls and email. Please believe your voice counts. Please believe that when enough of us raise our voices together at one time they do have an impact.

Cheney and his minions are absolutely not going to stop pushing for an even bigger disaster unless we stop them by speaking out with a louder voice. So we cannot let up ourselves even for an instant.

AND IF YOU LIKE KUCINICH ON THE ISSUES LET HIM KNOW

We would be remiss not to ask who other than Dennis Kucinich has shown more courage to speak out against the Iraq disaster before it even started? If you are asking yourself what you can do to encourage Dennis to continue to stand strong on the ISSUES, why not make a contribution, if you are so motivated.

Forward this message to everyone else you know.

Please take action NOW, so we can win all victories that are supposed to be ours, and forward this message to everyone else you know. Senator Barrack Obama and John Edwards is our only real hope for The future of Democracy.

ISRAEL A DEMOCRACY? SINCE WHEN, NEVER HAS BEEN, NEVER WILL BE. -- PALESTINE HAS THE RIGHT OF RETURN, ALWAYS HAS, ALWAYS WILL:

It is a violation of international law to collectively punish more than a million people for something they did not do. According to the Geneva Convention, to which it is a signatory, Israel actually has the obligation to ensure the well-being of the people on whom it has chosen to impose a military occupation for more than four decades.

Instead, it has shrugged off the law. It has ignored the repeated demands of the U.N. Security Council. It has dismissed the International Court of Justice in the Hague. What John Dugard, the U.N.'s special rapporteur on human rights in the occupied territories, refers to as the "carefully managed" strangulation of Gaza - in full view of an uncaring world - is explicitly part of its strategy. "The idea," said Dov Weisglass, an Israeli government advisor, "is to put the Palestinians on a diet, but not make them die of hunger."

An entire generation of Palestinians in Gaza is growing up stunted: physically and nutritionally stunted because they are not getting enough to eat; emotionally stunted because of the pressures of living in a virtual prison and facing the constant threat of destruction and displacement.

The powers of "Jewish supremacism". The oligarchs and the Zionists want total supremacy over our nation. Their puppet George Bush, just as in the Iraq war, is happy to serve these masters of the American political landscape. It is not just leaders of AIPAC that are being investigated for spying. George Bush has surrendered his presidency completely to this foreign power and shames every real American who has pride in our country.

NO MORE PUBLIC FUNDS, TAX DOLLARS, FOR ISRAEL SUPPORT !

We as citizens of the United States request that no further funding of a religious state with Our public funds continue. We request that no further military aid be given to a religious state. We also request a return of our funds. From the "Jewish State of Israel".

Our constitution specifically separates church & state. NONE of our tax dollars should be used in support of any religious institution, government or annex of such state.

They may have declared themselves a separate State, but our constitution strictly forbids using our public money or tax dollars from supporting such, and we demand that such practice discontinue immediately.

The UN has tried to make Israel responsible for their evil actions, but is always vetoed by the USA. If we don't bring fair, honest, & credible solutions to the table. Which means holding the culprits to pay for the injustice we all have witnessed, and you all denied and continue to. We know we will pay dearly for your mistakes, Bush/Cheney mistakes, and Israels mistakes, simply because of your unwavering support for a regime that is absolutely the worst in the region. We want America to be the America we knew, prior to the ambush of AIPAC and other such foreign influences. Will any of you stand up for the principles of consequence and truth... Regardless, we Americans know the truth, and when you all decide to face it, do something about it. We will stand with you. Otherwise you all will go down with the Ship. The ship that many are abandoning,rightfully so. The American people are getting ready to take back our Country from AIPAC, ISRAEL, and the ZIONIST movement. THE REAL "AXIS OF EVIL"..

Hillary is not the first politician in Washington to declare "Mission Accomplished" a little too soon.

Subject: "WAR FOR PROFIT" WILL NOT END WITH HILLARY, WHY? SPECIAL INTEREST MONEY!

Companies awarded multi-billions in contracts to rebuild Iraq and Afghanistan has been major campaign donors to President Bush, and their executives have had important political and military connections, according to a study released.

The study of more than 70 U.S. companies and individual contractors turned up more than $500,000 in donations to the president's 2000 campaign, more than they gave collectively to any other politician over the past dozen years.

Yes, 2000 campaign, the planning had begun back then.

Even before the war in Iraq began March 20, the Bush administration was considering plans to help rebuild the country after fighting ceased. According to news reports in early March, the U.S. Agency for International Development secretly asked six U.S. companies to submit bids for a $900 million government contract to repair and reconstruct water systems, roads, bridges, schools and hospitals in Iraq.

The six companies -- Bechtel Group Inc., Fluor Corp., Halliburton Co. subsidiary Kellogg, Brown & Root, Louis Berger Group Inc., Parsons Corp. and Washington Group International Inc. -- contributed a combined $3.6 million in individual, PAC and soft money donations between 1999 and 2002, the Center reported on its news site, CapitalEye.org. Sixty-six percent of that total went to Republicans.

The size and scope of the government contracts awarded to Halliburton in connection with the war in Iraq are significantly greater than was previously disclosed and demonstrate the U.S. military's increasing reliance on for-profit corporations to run its logistical operations. Independent experts estimate that as much as one-third of the monthly $3.9 billion cost of keeping U.S. troops in Iraq is going to independent contractors.

In addition, the company has earned about $705 million for an initial round of oil field rehabilitation work for the Army Corps of Engineers, a corps spokesman said.

Halliburton was headed by Vice President Dick Cheney before he resigned to run with Mr. Bush in 2000. How convenient. As convenient as Senator Wellstones death, Wellstone's airplane lacked the usual flight data recorder and a cockpit voice recorder, even though FAA spokesman Paul Takemoto said that the plane was supposed to be so equipped.

Another dropped investigation.

In addition to its Iraq contracts, Brown and Root has also earned $183 million from Operation Enduring Freedom, the military name for the war on terrorism and combat operations in Afghanistan, according to the Army's numbers.

At the end of the day, neither these companies nor their employees are bound by military justice.

A CONTRACTOR in Iraq has pleaded guilty to providing money, sex and designer watches to US officials in exchange for more than $US8 million ($10.8 million) in reconstruction contracts. No wonder they all want to visit so often.

First-class air tickets, real estate lots, weapons, new four-wheel-drive vehicles, cigars, designer watches, alcohol, prostitutes at Bloom's Baghdad villa and cash bribes, were provided.

Robert Stein, a civilian contractor who controlled $US82 million in reconstruction funds as the comptroller for the coalition's headquarters.

Stein, who had a previous conviction for fraud when he was hired, pleaded guilty to accepting bribes in February. He funneled money and favors from Bloom to other officials .

The contracts were paid with Iraqi funds held in the Development Fund for Iraq, which has been at the centre of many of the corruption scandals in Iraq. Looks like Iraqi's are victims again of the, American "War for Profiteers".

"No single agency supervised the contracting process for the government," Center executive director Charles Lewis said. "This situation alone shows how susceptible the contracting system is to waste, fraud and cronyism."

No one operated alone, nor did they operate with out paying Democrats also. It is just the fact that more went to Republicans. BUT corruption is corruption, appearing on both sides of the isle.

Special interest money comes with the tag of, you now owe me, and they pay and pay. It is always the tax payer losing in the end.

No accountability, no justice, no prosecution. No ethics or integrity.

Who now receives the Special interest money? Have any questions? Just vote NO at the polls.

Republicans, Democrats, Independents, Green Party, Conservative, Liberal, Black, White, Brown, Red, Yellow, Male, Female, or not sure. We are all Americans We need to pull together for the benefit of our Country, and to prevent more War.

Of all the candidates to date, the most promising for the average American and our interest, instead of Corporate or Foreign lobbies, or religious state.

Is a ticket of Obama & Edwards. Our children and their children will be paying for the mess of the last 7+ years, we have to change it.

No other candidate can live up to the Countries expectations.

Subject: SAME OLD BUSHIT

BUSH OR HILLARY---THE SAME POLICIES, FOREIGN OR DOMESTIC.

BUSH: SPYING ON US CITIZENS:

New reports in the past week have revealed how extensive the illegal spying operations conducted by the Bush administration on the people of this country have been -- and it started within five weeks of Bush taking office. Quest telecommunications CEO for instance, revealed that the administration had demanded the phone records of US citizens starting six months before the September 11 attack. The mass violations of civil rights and civil liberties carried out by this administration has outraged people across the United States.But not by some Senators that gave Bush a green light..

"HILLARY'S CELL PHONE SPYING TO BE PROBED "

Hillary Clinton over her position on government surveillance, capitalizing on allegations in a recent book that Clinton listened to a secretly recorded conversation between political opponents.
"Hillary Clinton's campaign hypocrisy continues to know no bounds. It is rather unbelievable that Clinton would listen in to conversations being conducted by political opponents, "Team Clinton can expect to see and hear this over and over again over the course of the next year."
Clinton and Bush, bow to AIPAC, accept special interest money, agreed on the WAR. Seem to agreed on dismantling the Constitution, both use illegal monitoring.
Foreign policy the same regarding the atrocities of Israel and human rights violations, and occupation.

VOTERS, we need change, not more of the same old Bushit. I believe we need the team of Obama & Edwards for 2008.

Subject: SPYING OPERATIONS??

New reports in the past week have revealed how extensive the illegal spying operations conducted by the Bush administration on the people of this country have been -- and it started within five weeks of Bush taking office. Quest telecommunications CEO for instance, revealed that the administration had demanded the phone records of US citizens starting six months before the September 11 attack. The mass violations of civil rights and civil liberties carried out by this administration has outraged people across the United States. The movement for impeachment is demanding that Bush and Cheney be held accountable for their gross violations of the constitution. Impeachment is an imperative.

The Washington Post, San Francisco Chronicle, UPI and other national and international media have carried major articles about the government's creation of small flying surveillance devices that look somewhat like dragonflies.

While there are those who would like to dismiss the implications of such spying, the fact is that if the government is intentionally conducting secret photographic or audio surveillance targeting people because they are engaged in public protest and First Amendment-protected activities, this would be a significant constitutional rights violation.

It is important to keep in perspective this kind of government action. The government's efforts at surveillance of the progressive movement are also intended to chill public participation in political action; they seek to intimidate their opponents. The purpose of surveillance against the anti-war movement is not to "protect" the country. Rather it is evidence that the Bush administration fears the mobilization of the people of the United States who have seen through the lies and blatantly illegal conduct of the government itself. In fact, it is unmistakable evidence that shows that the Bush White House fears the power of the people.

Take a stand against government repression. Help this movement grow. We will not be intimidated. We will be in the streets across the country on October 27 demanding an end to the war in Iraq and the necessary impeachment of Bush, Cheney and other responsible officials for high crimes and misdemeanors.

Vanessa Alarcon saw them while working at an antiwar rally in Lafayette Square last month.

"I heard someone say, 'Oh my god, look at those,'" the college senior from New York recalled. "I look up and I'm like, 'What the hell is that?' They looked kind of like dragonflies or little helicopters. But I mean, those are not insects."

Out in the crowd, Bernard Crane saw them, too.

"I'd never seen anything like it in my life," the Washington lawyer said. "They were large for dragonflies. I thought, 'Is that mechanical, or is that alive?'"

Robotic fliers have been used by the military since World War II, but in the past decade their numbers and level of sophistication have increased enormously. Defense Department documents describe nearly 100 different models in use today, some as tiny as birds, and some the size of small planes.

All told, the nation's fleet of flying robots logged more than 160,000 flight hours last year -- a more than fourfold increase since 2003. A recent report by the U.S. Army Command and General Staff College warned that if traffic rules are not clarified soon, the glut of unmanned vehicles "could render military airspace chaotic and potentially dangerous."

The Office of the Director of National Intelligence, the Department of Homeland Security and the Secret Service also declined to discuss the topic.

"I don't want people to get paranoid, but what can I say?" - "Cellphone cameras are already everywhere. It's not that much different."

Hillary is not the first politician in Washington to declare "Mission Accomplished" a little too soon.

Subject: OBAMA--EDWARDS OR EDWARDS--OBAMA THE TEAM AMERICA NEEDS.

I did my Research on this before I would sent it out and it is listed at the bottom.

Edwards and Obama or Vs/Vs

Little History Lesson

Answer all the questions before looking at the answers.

Who said it?

1) "We're going to take things away from you on behalf of the common good."

A. Karl Marx
B. Adolph Hitler
C. Joseph Stalin
D. None of the above

2) "It's time for a new beginning, for an end to government of the few, by the few, and for the few...... And to replace it with shared responsibility for shared prosperity."

A. Lenin
B. Mussolini
C. Idi Amin
D. None of the Above

3) "(We) ...can't just let business as usual go on, and that means something has to be taken away from some people."

A. &n bsp;Nikita Khrushev
B. Josef Goebbels
C. Boris Yeltsin

D. None of the above

4) "We have to build a political consensus and that requires people to give up a little bit of their own ... in order to create this common ground."

A. Mao Tse Dung
B. Hugo Chavez
C. Kim Jong Il
D. None of the above

5) "I certainly think the free-market has failed."

A. Karl Marx
B. Lenin
C. Molotov
D. None of the above

6) "I think it's time to send a clear message to what has become the most profitable sector in (the) entire economy that they are being watched."

A. Pinochet
B. Milos evic
C. Saddam Hussein
D . None of the above

Scroll down for answers

Answers

(1) D. None of the above. Statement was made by Hillary Clinton 6/29/2004
(2) D. None of the above. Statement was m ade by Hillary Clinton 5/29/2007

(3) D. None of the above. Statement was made by Hillary Clinton 6/4/2007

(4) D. None of the above. Statement was made by Hillary Clinton 6/4/2007

(5) D. None of the above. Statement was made by Hillary Clinton 6/4/2007

(6) D. None of the above. Statement was made by Hillary Clinton 9/2/2005

I did verify these and it is true. I'm attaching the actual speech or article quoting the speech here so you can see for yourself. Some I actually got from her website. So I'm trying to be as fair as possible.

1. http://www.freerepublic.com/focus/f-news/1162872/posts

2.http://www.hillaryclinton.com/news/speech/view/?id=1839

3.http://transcripts.cnn.com/TRANSCRIPTS/0706/04/sitroom.03.html

4.http://transcripts.cnn.com/TRANSCRIPTS/0706/04/sitroom.03.html

5.http://transcripts.cnn.com/TRANSCRIPTS/0706/04/sitroom.03.html

6.This passage is from a September 2, 2005 appearance by Sen. Clinton in front of constituents in Elmira Heights, NY.

Subject: PARANOIA BY US POLITICIANS, TO AVOID THE EXPOSURE OF CORRUPTION ,AND WAR PROFITEERING, THREATEN OUR DEMOCRACY AND CONSTITUTION.

New target for the administration's domestic operations -- Fifth Columnists, supposedly disloyal Americans, Dissidents who are tagged as sympathizers and collaborators with the enemy.

"I stand by this President's ability, inherent to being Commander in Chief, to find out about Fifth Column movements, and I don't think you need a warrant to do that," Graham added, volunteering to work with the administration to draft guidelines for how best to neutralize this alleged threat.

The Bush administration may already be contemplating what to do with Americans who are deemed insufficiently loyal or who disseminate information that may be considered helpful to the enemy.

Top U.S. officials have cited the need to challenge news that undercuts Bush's actions as a key front in defeating the terrorists, who are aided by "news informers".

127 Journalist killed in Iraq. Were they neutralized? Were they an alleged threat, because of reporting the truth? The truth, such as on Blackwater killers reported as such, way back in 2005.

Plus, there was that curious development in January when the Army Corps of Engineers awarded Halliburton subsidiary Kellogg Brown & Root a $385 million contract to construct detention centers somewhere in the United States, to support the rapid development of new programs.

Phrase "rapid development of new programs" and what kind of programs would require a major expansion of detention centers, each capable of holding 5,000 people. They declined to elaborate on what these "new programs" might be. Detention centers would be used to detain American citizens if the Bush administration were to declare martial law. The reference to a "rapid action revision" and the KBR contract's contemplation of "rapid development of new programs" have raised eyebrows about why this sudden need for urgency. The National Security Agency, which has been engaging in surveillance of U.S. citizens without court-approved warrants, in apparent violation of the Foreign Intelligence Security Act. Bush approved the program of warrant less wiretaps shortly after 911.

With this expanded surveillance, the government's list of terrorist suspects is rapidly swelling.

The combination of the Bush administration's expansive reading of its own power and its insistence on extraordinary secrecy has raised the alarm of civil libertarians when contemplating how far the Pentagon might go in involving itself in domestic matters.

There are concerns over how the Pentagon judges "threats" and who falls under the category "those who would harm us." A Pentagon official said the Counterintelligence Field Activity's TALON program has amassed files on antiwar protesters.

NBC News revealed the existence of a secret 400-page Pentagon document listing 1,500 "suspicious incidents" over a 10-month period, including dozens of small antiwar demonstrations that were classified as a "threat."

The Pentagon plan also includes a strategy for taking over the Internet and controlling the flow of information, viewing the Web as a potential military adversary. The "roadmap" speaks of "fighting the net," and implies that the Internet is the equivalent of "an enemy weapons system."

This claimed authority is based on the assertion that the United States is at war and the American homeland is part of the battlefield.

Bush's now open assertions that he is using his "plenary" – or unlimited – powers as Commander in Chief for the duration of the indefinite War on Terror, Americans can no longer trust that their constitutional rights protect them from government actions. The American people might legitimately ask exactly what the Bush administration means by the "rapid development of new programs," which might require the construction of a new network of detention camps.

Dissidents are being targeted; most of the theories rest upon circumstantial evidence and long stretches of the imagination. Will more journalist die, end up in jail, or just disappear? Or forced to retire, or let go after character assassination, we have witnessed some of these scenarios.

President George W. Bush, backed by a nearly united Republican Party, took the US into war against Iraq. The Bush administration, resolutely supported by a phalanx of neocon ivory tower warriors, GOP-minded pundits, and grassroots conservative activists, undertook to build democracy in Mesopotamia. For nearly three years a right-wing Greek chorus has spouted the president's praises as he insisted that all was well with America's newest military venture in the Mideast.

Yet things haven't worked out as expected. However, war supporters insist that the problems have nothing to do with the brilliant leadership exercised by the valiant President Bush. To the contrary, it is someone else's fault. Indeed, it is everyone else's fault. At least, it is the fault of anyone who has dared criticize the valiant president and his brilliant leadership.

The latest manifestation of this attitude is the oft-repeated argument that all good patriots must back the "surge," the president's belated, half-hearted escalation in Iraq. To oppose the Bush plan, to even criticize it, is to undercut America's troops and give aid and comfort to America's enemies. To advocate another course, any alternative course, is to invite jihadists to terrorize the US homeland.

Indeed, as the situation in Iraq has worsened, the tendency to ring the wagons and demand absolute obedience has increased. The atmosphere in some quarters of the dwindling pro-war caucus is akin to that of the Führer bunker in early 1945. The problem is not any failure of the supreme leader or his vision, but the inconstancy of his lieutenants and the wimpishness of his people. Victory is a simple matter of WILL.

For instance, Paul Morin, national commander of the National Legion, circulated an opinion piece entitled "Iraq Victory Requires Renewed Resolve." Morin's message was simple. While Winston Churchill advocated resolve, "America's stiff upper lip is starting to quiver." People need to "stand united in their support of the global war on terrorism," in which he apparently included Iraq. To not do so would be to "cut and run," or "Surrender Somalia-style."

Apparently victory is ours if only we close our eyes, click our heels, and say "George Bush" three times. Explained Morin: "Give our soldiers the strength of a galvanized homefront so we can win the peace in Iraq." Columnist Paul Greenberg made the same contention: "Unless the homefront stands united, no new general in Iraq, even one with a new strategy that has begun to produce results, will be able to stave off defeat." Sen. Lindsey Graham (R-SC) has exclaimed: "Any [legislative] resolution that could be construed by American forces that Congress has lost faith in their ability to be successful in Iraq should be rejected because it rings of defeatism at a time when we should be focused on victory." Commentator Quin Hillyer said "What is lacking in Iraq is not winnability but will."

Liz Cheney, vice presidential daughter and former assistant secretary of state, recently made the same "mind over matter" assertion in the Washington Post: "American troops will win if we show even one-tenth the courage here at home that they show every day on the battlefield." So forget the idea of dissenting from failed policies from a failed president. Argued Cheney: "It's time for everyone – Republicans and Democrats – to stop trying to find ways for America to quit. Victory is the only option. We must have the fortitude and the courage to do what it takes. In the words of Winston Churchill, we must deserve victory. We must be in it to win."

Her father has offered a similar argument. Vice President Richard Cheney contended: "we have to have the stomach to finish the task." Our adversaries "say the United States doesn't have the stomach for the fight." Not that he had the stomach to even start a similar task in Vietnam – a conflict he worked hard to avoid because, as he later explained, he "had other priorities." But never mind. (Moving increasingly distant from reality and the truth, he recently denounced as "hogwash" the question whether congressional Republicans "are now seriously questioning your credibility, because of the blunders and the failures." Never mind the bump, Mr. Vice President. The Titanic is unsinkable.)

Since many war-hawks believe that all they have to do is believe in the president to ensure victory in Iraq, they are furious with just about everyone for turning into gutless wimps. Much of their ire is directed against legislators who oppose sending an additional 21,500 Marines and soldiers to Iraq. (In fact, Stanley Kurtz of the Hudson Institute blamed the opposition of Democratic doves – an impotent minority for years – for making "it tough for the administration to admit errors on troop strength and correct course" from the very beginning. Under this theory, the new Democratic majority has only made an existing bad situation worse.)

The Democrats have been divided between those who support passing a non-binding resolution of disapproval and those who want to cut off funds. In practice, the Democratic majority is too divided to stop the war, a division which the White House has exploited. Noted House Speaker Nancy Pelosi: "The president knows that because the troops are in harm's way that we won't cut off the resources. That's why he's moving so quickly to put them in harm's way."

Senate Foreign Relations Committee Chairman Joseph Biden has remained hopeful that something good will come from Congress's efforts: "If you really want to change the situation on the ground, demonstrate to the president that he's on his own. That will spark real change." Of course, even President Bush, long lost in a fantasy world, presumably finally realizes that he's on his own. But that obviously doesn't matter to him.

The president appears to be committed to his policy, irrespective of consequences. Certainly the administration does not plan on being deterred by congressional displeasure. Vice President Cheney was dismissive: "in terms of this effort, the president has made his decision. We've consulted extensively with [legislators]. We'll continue to consult with the Congress. But the fact of the matter is, we need to get the job done."

The first response of hawks to Democratic attacks was silly: don't criticize our plan without offering yours. For instance, the Washington Examiner editorialized that "It's irresponsible in the extreme to reject Bush's last ditch attempt to stabilize Iraq out of hand without suggesting a better way to win." Actually, it's quite easy to reject a half-baked plan that mimics past strategies which have failed, an approach that would be administered by the same inept officials responsible for today's chaos and violence. Moreover, there may be no better way to win. Indeed, creating a stable, pro-American democracy in Iraq may never have been realistic.

In a similar vein, Senate Minority Leader Mitch McConnell denounced the Democrats's attempt "to try to micromanage" battlefield tactics: "You can't run a war by a committee of, you know, 435 in the House and 100 in the Senate." Similarly, editorialized the Wall Street Journal: "What we are witnessing is a Federalist

Papers illustration of criticism and micromanagement without responsibility." Actually, that sounds more like the administration's conduct of the war. The president's flight from responsibility for Iraq is what led to the Democratic victory last November and the new Democratic majority's attempt to stop the Bush escalation.

So it seems likely that congressional opposition will have no practical impact on the administration's course. But the Democrats don't have to actually do anything to anger the neocons and other deskbound warriors. The possibility that Congress might merely state the obvious – Iraq is a bloody mess and the proposed "surge" is an under-manned fraud – has left the war caucus apoplectic.

For instance, "The Democrats are going to have to make a choice here," said presidential press secretary Tony Snow: "No. 1, do you want Iraq to succeed?" Sometime Republican candidate and office-holder Howard Kaloogian charged in summer 2004: Democrats "have used some of the most irresponsible language in seeking to advance their liberal political goals by trying to divide our nation and erode support for our military and the war effort." Columnist David Limbaugh has complained about "Democrats undermining our war effort." Democratic legislators are "favoring defeat over victory in the Iraqi theater," contended the Center for Security Policy. Columnist Mona Charen said that "the Democrats do not wish to win in Iraq and will do nothing to further the cause of victory."

Blogger and radio talk show host Hugh Hewitt sharply denounced congressional resolutions of disapproval as intended "to undercut the war, endanger the troops and weaken the presidency." Internet columnist Lorie Byrd argued that "There is a difference, however, between disagreement over methods and implementation, and the more basic disagreement over whether or not the final goal is to pursue victory, rather than defeat through surrender."

However, what the Democrats want really doesn't matter. Whether or not they desire victory, merely criticizing the administration means that they are making victory impossible. Asked Byrd: "If it were clear to the Iraqi people that politicians in DC were committed to finishing the mission in Iraq, would the attitude of the people be different? If politicians and antiwar activists had not accused our own troops of engaging in torture, and worse, would world opinion, and specifically the opinion of the Iraqi people, be different?" (What she really meant, of course, is what if politicians and antiwar activists had not stated the sad truth obvious to all that some troops had murdered and tortured Iraqis?, but never mind the facts.)

It's no longer just Democrats who pose a problem for the avid warmongers, however. Republican legislators are growing increasingly uneasy as well.

For the biggest war enthusiasts, GOP hostility is the toughest burden to bear. It no longer is just Sen. Chuck Hagel (R-Neb.), who voted to authorize war but soon began criticizing the administration's gross mismanagement. Now even the ultimate establishment paladin, Sen. Richard Lugar (R-Ind.), has admitted: "I am not confident that President Bush's plan will succeed." Horrors. The shame. The outrage.

In November 2005 blogger Will Malven denounced Republican Senators who simply voted to mandate that the executive issue a quarterly report on Iraq: "What is really disgusting is that, not only have the Republicans stabbed President Bush in the back, but by expressing distrust in the Iraqi efforts, they endangered the American troops by added defeatist propaganda to the terrorist's arsenal." Now several Republican legislators are preparing to vote to formally criticize the administration's escalation plan.

Hugh Hewitt has launched an effort to deny campaign funds to any Republican who backs a resolution criticizing the administration's escalation. He is urging people to promise to close their wallets to the National Republican Senatorial Committee unless the chairman, "Senator Ensign, commits in writing that none of the funds of the NRSC will go to support the reelection of any senator supporting the non-binding resolution."

It is hard to be a war-hawk irrespective of consequences when so many elected officials turn out to be closet peaceniks. And even worse, traitorous closet peaceniks.

To many war enthusiasts, criticism, any criticism, is the same as treason. Defense Secretary Robert Gates testified that a resolution of disapproval "emboldens the enemy and our adversaries." Indeed, he added, "any indication of flagging will in the United States gives encouragement to those folks." The vice president said that the push for withdrawal "validates the strategy of the terrorists." An article by Ann Coulter was entitled: "The Democratic Party: A Vast Sleeper Cell." Hewitt contended: "Many Democrats are willing to encourage the enemy if it means hurting George W. Bush."

Sen. Graham argued, "if you think the US is doomed to fail, please remember that the enemy is listening." Rep. Sam Johnson (R-Tex.) complained a year ago that "Any talk, even so much as a murmur, of leaving now or political timelines just emboldens the enemy." Publisher Edward Daley termed the Democrats "The Party of Treason" and contended that criticism "amounts to treason, as it does indeed give 'aid and comfort' to our enemies, and further endangers the lives" of US personnel.

"The terrorists couldn't have better allies than certain politicians here in the US," declared Melanie Morgan of Move America Forward. Washington Times columnist Diana West said that any congressional vote against the war "goes straight to our enemies, who will hunker down to wait for a divided America to up and crumble." Mark Alexander, publisher of The Patriot Post, an internet newsletter, declared that stating doubts about victory in Iraq "is not just unpatriotic, it is downright traitorous."

Contended the Wall Street Journal: "Of course the enemy would take comfort from any Senate declaration that Mr. Bush lacks domestic support." John Raese, who unsuccessfully opposed Robert Byrd (D-W.Va.) last November, charged that the latter's votes to withdraw

US troops "give comfort to the enemy." Oliver North denounced "defeatists," claiming that Democratic criticism "has unquestionably emboldened our adversaries and disheartened our allies overseas." Internet columnist Doug Patton bluntly described "the actions of liberals" as "treason."

Hugh Hewitt, a de facto member of President Bush's personal staff, contended that "Democrats are willing to encourage the enemy," that is, increase the latter's "will to fight on, and their courage to do so even in the face of the arrival of reinforcements. It also means to increase – substantially – the likelihood of redoubled and retripled efforts on their part to kill American soldiers, sailors, airmen and Marines."

In the same vein, declared the Center for Security Policy, "It is hard to imagine a greater incentive to more attacks against Iraqi civilians, security personnel, government officials and their families – and, yes, against our own and other Coalition forces" than Democratic criticism. The Center added ominously: "we must also hold accountable those who are, in effect, rewarding our enemies." Radio talk show host Michael Reagan was more specific: Democratic National Committee Chairman "Howard Dean should be arrested and hung for treason or put in a hole until the end of the Iraq war."

Moreover, any criticism of Bush administration failures is believed to axiomatically hurt the troops. Rep. Joe Wilson (R-S.C.) said that "it is just inconceivable and truly incorrigible that in the midst of the war, that the Democratic leaders would be conducting guerrilla warfare on American troops." Rep. Johnson charged: "It hurts to think what the men and women in harm's way would believe when they heard the news that someone in Congress was not behind America's mission."

The vice president said that any resolution would be "detrimental from the standpoint of the troops." In the view of the Wall Street Journal, a simple congressional resolution disapproving of the war "undermines public support for the Iraq effort." Of course, the

Journal added, "all of this undermines the morale of the military and makes their task that much harder on the ground." Michael Reagan charged that Democrats have been "undermining the valiant efforts of our servicemen and women." Lorie Byrd said simply that Democratic statements "declaring Iraq a failure and accusing US troops of improper behavior has affected their morale."

Of course, everything is the media's fault. Blogger Steve Schippert has denounced "anti-military media coverage developed during the Vietnam era and skillfully maintained and nearly perfected since then." Lorie Byrd complained about "one-sided reporting," that "When the war is going well, it is simply not considered news." (She doesn't point to any time when the occupation was going well, but never mind.) In AIMReport Marilyn Brannan asked: "Will the Media defeat the US in Iraq?" Washington Times Editorial Page Editor Tony Blankley admitted to being "filled with a fury that we have a system of journalism that permits people with such mentalities to poison the minds of the world with their malice."

Gen. Peter Pace, chairman of the Joint Chiefs of Staff, said press negativity "is absolutely detrimental to the morale of our forces." Michael Novak of the American Enterprise Institute contended that what "we have discovered in Iraq is the weakest link in the ability of the United States to sustain military operations overs. That link is the US media. They are the Islamists' best friends." Col. Jeffrey Snow, who commands a brigade in Baghdad, complained that "when the news is not balanced and it's always bad, that clearly leads to negative perceptions back home."

However, it turns out that the US media is not only omnipresent and all-powerful in America. US journalists apparently control events in Iraq itself. Byrd asked: "If all the successes of American troops in Iraq had been reported as studiously as the setbacks, would terrorists have been able to convince their young, impressionable followers that they were winning?" Indeed, she went even further, wondering "if the rallying cry [of the Iraq war to jihadists] was a result of the war itself or if it was the result of the media interpretation of the war presented through anti-American media outlets like BBC, al-Jazeera and CNN International as a losing effort in which Christian American troops were torturing and murdering innocent Muslims?"

Townhall.com columnist Todd Manzi charged: "We know how important the will of the American people is regarding the war. Doesn't the will of the terrorists matter also? If their cause looks lost, they will attack less. If they think they have a chance to win, they will attack more. The irresponsible, antiwar-biased reporting from the Associated Press ... can only have encouraged our enemy to keep trying. Terrorists may have been given the false hope that all is not lost for them."

Perhaps most amazing of all, it turns out that even when journalists are correct, they are at fault. As Stanley Kurtz of the Hudson Institute explained on National Review online:

"[C]onservative distrust of the media's very real bias has inclined us to dismiss reports about problems in Iraq that are real.

"In the end, I think the media bears fundamental responsibility for this. Had they been less-biased – had they reported acts of heroism and the many good things we have done in Iraq – I think conservatives would actually have taken their report of the problems in Iraq more seriously. In effect, the media's consistent liberal bias discredits even its valid reports."

Finally, the general population is to blame. Melanie Morgan complained that American troops are "being undermined here at home by shameful, guilt-ridden, spineless folks in the antiwar crowd." Former House Speaker Denny Hastert charged that war critics would "prefer that the United States surrender to terrorists." Sen. Graham lauded the administration's investigation of domestic protestors: "The administration has not only the right, but the duty, in my opinion, to pursue Fifth Column movements."

David Horowitz of the Center for the Study of Popular Culture warned: "the Fifth Column in this country has attempted to sabotage America's war in Iraq." Wade Zirkle, chairman of Vets for Freedom Action Fund, denounced "defeatism" and "defeatist radicals." Book author Jeffrey Lord criticized "the chorus of modern day Copperheads doing their best to undermine America's will."

In 2005 the American Legion blasted all antiwar "public protests" and "media events." National commander Thomas Cadmus explained: "The American Legion will stand against anyone and any group that would demoralize our troops, or worse, endanger their lives by encouraging terrorists to continue their cowardly attacks against freedom-loving peoples."

Even worse is the disreputable role of average Americans. Stanley Kurtz complained that "the constraints of domestic American public opinion do not match up to what is actually needed to bring stability and democracy to a country like Iraq." Roll Call's Morton Kondracke was even blunter: "President Bush bet his presidency – and America's world leadership – on the war in Iraq. Tragically, it looks as though he bit off more than the American people were willing to chew." Ungrateful plebeians, rejecting the war generously provided for them by their betters.

The consistent attempt at blame-shifting by the most extreme hawks is truly amazing. People who normally denounce those who refuse to take responsibility for their actions, who act like victims, who blame everyone else for their mistakes, are engaging in precisely the same behavior. Iraq? Problems? Not our fault. We dreamed up a truly fabulous little war. It's really gone quite well, filled with good news – you know, increased cell phone use, more-frequent trash pick-ups, new school openings. What of thousands of dead Americans and tens of thousands of dead Iraqis? The Democrats, the media, and the people are to blame. If they didn't say anything about the problems, the problems wouldn't exist. At least, no one in Iraq would know that things weren't going as well as the president claimed if American journalists did their duty and parroted administration claims. After all, if no reporter witnesses an IED attack on an American convoy or a car bombing in an Iraqi market, it doesn't exist. By telling the truth, war critics are a bunch of wimps, cowards, defeatists, and traitors, undercutting the US and aiding America's enemies.

It's a wonderful tale. Too bad it is completely false.

President George W. Bush peopled his administration with officials who had long desired to initiate war against Iraq. After 9/11, his administration inaugurated a consistently deceptive, misleading campaign to make the case for war. Essentially everything he and his officials said about WMDs and Iraq's terrorist connections were false. Professed concern for democracy was undercut by the fact that the president waited a year after taking office to mention Iraq, and pressed for action only long after the worst humanitarian excesses had occurred.

Once at war, the administration blundered at every turn. Blinded by overweening hubris, military and political officials alike made a succession of bad decisions that resulted in a violent breakdown of Iraqi society, a worsening insurgency, and a fracturing of the already-divided polity. Even as the situation deteriorated, the president and his aides denied reality and continued to paint a rosey scenario. Constant promises of turning points turned out to be constantly false.

Along the way the administration's performance failed to meet basic levels of competence. Reconstruction efforts were a corrupt disaster. The administration provided too few troops and too little equipment (such as body armor and armored vehicles). Yet the president was loudly cheered on by his war-mongering propaganda chorus, which demonized anyone who dared question the imminent establishment of a peaceful, liberal, pro-American, democratic paradise along the Euphrates.

Despite desperate attempts to sugar-coat the situation in Iraq, the bad news eventually became evident to even America's most isolated partisan – the president. With many of the neocon architects of the war now jumping ship, denying any responsibility for anything that has happened, the administration concocted the so-called surge.

Yet for all of the fanfare, the administration's plan is a paltry effort. Total US forces will remain under the 165,000 peak more than a year ago, as well as far below the number indicated by current anti-insurgency doctrine, developed in part by Gen. Petraeus, newly entrusted with the war effort.

Moreover, the latest plan mimics the recent "surge" of American troops in Baghdad, which did little to moderate the far more pronounced "surge" in sectarian killings. In short, few serious analysts expect any permanent benefit from the administration's newest escalation. It is far too modest to have much chance of affecting Iraq's ultimate course.

Nor, apparently, do some administration officials privately expect the policy to succeed. Late last month NBC reported that one Bush aide "admitted to us today that this surge option is more of a political decision than a military one because the American people have run out of patience and President Bush is running out of time to achieve some kind of success in Iraq." That is, the Bush escalation is essentially a PR gimic, a desperate attempt to hold off the growing mob of disaffected Americans before they besiege the White House.

It comes as no surprise, then, that support for both the president and the war among the public and even the military has fallen. A recent Military Times poll found that only 35 percent of respondents approved of Bush's handling of Iraq. In just two year the number believing that success is likely has dropped from 83 percent to 50 percent.

The problem is not defeatists and traitors, whether in the Democratic Party, media, or elsewhere. It is the reality on the ground, which has proved to be so very different than that promised by the president back during the "mission accomplished" days. It is a reality that even the president hinted at last December when he argued: "We're not winning, we're not losing."

Even so, the uber-hawks say that to not genuflect when the president and his aides walk by is to back defeat. To not lustily cheer the new program, assert that it will achieve victory forthwith, and shout administration hosannahs from the treetops is treason.

It matters not what the president proposes to do. The president, wrong about Iraq at every point so far, nevertheless must be treated as if he was never wrong. The president's plan, though reminiscent of other failed initiatives, must be treated as if it had been brought down from God by Moses, along with the Ten Commandments.

Must democracy be built on deceit? What the war's cheerleaders are really saying is that it doesn't matter how the conflict is going. We must lie to the public, our troops, and the rest of the world. We must claim that everything is peachy-keen and jim-dandy – just wonderful, thank you! – no matter what is happening.

Moreover, we cannot hold the administration accountable for its manifold mistakes. Never mind that the president and his aides have been uniformly arrogant, ignorant, deceitful, and incompetent. No ill word must pass our lips about their conduct. We must not criticize them even if their past failures make future success unlikely. After all, given the president's consistent mismanagement of the war so far, who – other than war propagandists who have tied themselves to his administration – could have any confidence in his ability to perform better in the future? But to make this point is unpatriotic, even treasonous.

Conservatives once criticized unnecessary wars and the mismanagement of unnecessary wars. During President Bill Clinton's misguided adventure in Kosovo, Rush Limbaugh, Michael Savage, Brent Bozell III, Angelo Codevilla, Tom Delay, Sean Hannity, Bill Bennett, and Joe Scarborough were just a few of the conservative luminaries who criticized the war even as it was being fought. And they were vilified by the Clinton administration and its hawkish supporters for being insufficiently patriotic.

But Sen. Robert Taft (R-Ohio) answered both the Democratic warmongers of 1999 and today's conservative war caucus when he spoke on December 19, 1941, less than two weeks after the attack on Pearl Harbor: "As a matter of general principle, I believe there can be no doubt that criticism in time of war is essential to the maintenance of any kind of democratic government."

He added:

"[T]oo many people desire to suppress criticism simply because they think that it will give some comfort to the enemy to know that there is such criticism. If that comfort makes the enemy feel better for a few moments, they are welcome to it as far as I am concerned, because the maintenance of the right of criticism in the long run will do the country maintaining it a great deal more good than it will do the enemy, and will prevent mistakes which might otherwise occur."

The Bush administration and its coterie of war supporters have squandered the trust of the American people. Their misjudgments, mistakes, and deceits have resulted in thousands of dead and maimed Americans while turning Iraq into a vortex of sectarian violence and increasing the threat of global terrorism. The architects and advocates of this war should – indeed, must – be criticized. Our responsibility as citizens in a democratic republic demand no less. However painful dissent might be in a time of war, the cost to America of shutting off debate would be far greater.

Subject: DISFUCNTIONAL GOVERNMENT and ILLEGAL IMMIGRATION.

AMERICA: NOW A DISFUCTIONAL GOVERNMENT.

It seems that 85% of the American People are opposed to illegal immigration, and all the problems that it causes on us, and our Country.

Yet, you have allowed and supported the illegal occupation by Israel, that illegally occupies Palestine, and Arab lands of Lebanon, Jordan, and Egypt. You neo-cons have supported the human rights violations for 60 years.

You all want to call it, Christianity, that there is a God given right to make these decisions. You do not recognize the wrongs of the Zionist movement, Political Preachers.

 Now, we witness Catholicism supporting the Illegal immigation from Mexico. Support another Amnesty Bill, and the detection centers For Americans that pose decent, being built by the Present administration.

What is the difference here or there, wrong is Wrong. Violation of our laws or international Laws. Should any have been ignored.

Well now, many of us only see the hypocrisy of the decisions made in the interest of wealth, and control. We do not see any of those governments fascist decisions as being Moral or any real justification.

We need to stop all the foreign aid to rogue states, such as Israel, and assist our border countries, so that they can compete from their own home land.

We need to respect resolutions rightfully passed by the UN, rather then to veto them in the interest of special interest money received by each government official.

We need complete change.

THE AMERICAN GOVERNMENT AND POLITICS, HAVE CHANGED DRASTICALLY, OVER THE LAST SEVEN YEARS.

FROM: MORAL VALUES, ETHICS, AND INTEGRITY.

TO: PROPAGANDA, RETHORIC, AND FACIST AGENDA.

We need immediate change. We will never regain our standing in the World. But a little self-respect from our own people would be a start.

The only way to begin is a different course, and one with the American peoples interest, not special interest groups, corporations & far right fanatics. Foreign or domestic as the Nations objective.

We need Obama & Edwards for change.

Bring our troops home, no more Wars, no more War for profit, or False devine doctrine policies.

A Foreign Policy of mind our own business, let the Inter-national organizations take care of their business.

A policy of complying with the Law would help the most. Unlike what we see each day now!!

"The question really is whether Congress should toss out chunks of the Constitution because Mr. Bush finds them inconvenient and some Democrats are afraid to look soft on terrorism... This provision is not primarily about protecting patriotic businessmen, as Mr. Bush claims. It's about ensuring that Mr. Bush and his aides never have to go to court to explain how many laws they've broken. It is a collusion between lawmakers and the White House that means that no one is ever held accountable."

So the White House is putting enormous pressure on Congress to give the phone companies retroactive immunity for all the laws they broke spying on innocent Americans. And some key Democrats are ready to go along!

It is imperative that all Americans see all votes from our representatives, see all Campaign contributions taken by all.

News reports indicate that Democratic senators agreed to give phone companies retroactive immunity after the Bush administration presented a one-sided case that these companies "acted in good faith." Of course that is after the exchange of millions.

That's ridiculous. A judge appointed by President Bush Sr. wrote an opinion finding that "AT&T cannot seriously contend that a reasonable entity in its position could have believed that the alleged domestic dragnet was legal."

The bottom line is that President Bush is trying to cover up his own lawbreaking with this immunity.

We need Congress to stop him. Senator Chris Dodd has courageously vowed to block this bill if the immunity provision is not taken out. We need to make sure other members of Congress come out and support his strong stand.

WHAT HE DOES BEFORE THE CAMERAS, CAMPAIGNING, AND PUSHING HIS AGENDA.

WHAT IS REAL OFF CAMERA, THE RESULTS OF HIS, TWISTED CAMPAIGN AND AGENDA.

Ronald L. Waldron

END THE WAR, END THE MURDER. OVER ONE MILLION
INNOCENT CIVILIANS, WOMEN & CHILDREN KILLED.
RANDOM KILLING, GIVEN IMMUNITY. WHY???

IF YOU LIKE WAR IN IRAQ, YOU WILL LOVE WAR ON IRAN :

Fact Sheets of Iran-US Standoff: Twenty Reasons against Sanctions and Military Intervention in Iran:

Four years since the US-UK led illegal invasion of Iraq, which has brought the ongoing catastrophe for Iraqi people, all peace loving people and antiwar organizations in the world are appalled by the current Iran-US standoff that has a shocking resemblance to the run-up to the invasion of Iraq. The same neo-conservatives and hawks, headed by Dick Cheney in Washington, who championed the cause of invasion of Iraq, are now shamelessly calling for a military attack on Iran. The same Israeli lobby which pushed for the invasion of Iraq, is now pushing for a military attack on Iran. The same strategy of lies and distortions which was used to dupe the international community and soften it up for the invasion of Iraq, is again used to pave the way for another illegal pre-emptive war of aggression against Iran. As in the case of Iraq, the UN Security Council Resolutions against Iran, obtained by massive US pressure and coercion, would provide a veneer of legitimacy for such an attack.

Contrary to the myth created by the western media, it is not Iran, but the US and its European allies which are defying the overwhelming majority of the international community, in that, they have resisted the call to enter into direct, immediate and comprehensive negotiations with Iran without any pre-conditions. The US and its European allies show their lack of good faith in a diplomatic solution to the standoff by demanding that Iran concede the main point of negotiations, namely, suspension of enrichment of uranium which is

Iran's legitimate right under the Non-Proliferation Treaty, before the negotiations actually start.

Here, we examine and debunk the common myths and charges against Iran and provide a list of twenty reasons to oppose sanctions and military intervention in Iran. The Campaign Against Sanctions and Military Intervention in Iran (CASMII) calls for immediate and direct negotiations between the US and Iran without any pre-conditions in order to avert a new even more horrifying catastrophe in the Middle East.

IRAN'S NUCLEAR PROGRAMME: FACTS AND LIES

1. There is no evidence of a nuclear weapons programme in Iran. The US and Israel pressure Iran to prove that it is not hiding a nuclear weapons programme. This demand is logically impossible to satisfy and only serves to make diplomacy fail in order to force regime change. Numerous intrusive and snap visits by International Atomic Energy Agency (IAEA) inspectors, totalling more than 2,700 person-hours of inspection, have failed to produce any shred of evidence for a weapons programme in Iran. Traces of highly enriched uranium found at Natanz in 2004, were determined by IAEA to have come with imported centrifuges.

In June 2005, Bruno Pellaud, former IAEA Deputy Director-General for safeguards, was asked by Swissinfo if Iran was intent on building a nuclear bomb. He replied: "My impression is not. My view is based on the fact that Iran took a major gamble in December 2003 by allowing a much more intrusive capability to the IAEA. If Iran had had a military programme they would not have allowed the IAEA to come under this Additional Protocol. They did not have to." Even the ex-British Foreign Minister, Jack Straw, admitted on 9/4/2006 that "there is no smoking gun and therefore no justification for a military attack". Still, for the US the absence of evidence is not evidence of absence.

2. Iran's need for nuclear power generation is real. Even when Iran's population was one-third of what it is today, Dick Cheney, Donald Rumsfeld and Paul Wolfowitz, negotiating on behalf of President Gerald Ford, persuaded the former Shah that Iran needed nuclear power and over twenty nuclear reactors. [1] Today Iran's electricity output forecast falls so much short of projected needs that even concerns over the preservation of historic sites did not impede Tehran's plans to dam a river near the national heritage ruins near Pasargad. With Iran's population of 70 million fast growing, and its oil resources fast depleting, Iran will be a net importer of oil productions in just over a decade from now. Nuclear energy is thus a realistic and viable solution for electricity generation in the country.

3. The "crisis" over Iran's nuclear programme lacks the urgency claimed by Washington. Even if it were to militarize its nuclear programme, for which there is no evidence at all, Iran would be many years away from mastering the technology, giving proliferation concerns ample time to be resolved by negotiation. Weapons grade uranium must be enriched at least to 85%. A 2005 CIA report determined that it could take Iran 10 years to achieve this level of enrichment. Many independent nuclear experts have stated that Iran would face formidable technical obstacles if it tried to enrich uranium beyond the 3.5% required for electricity generation. According to Dr Frank Barnaby of the Oxford Research Group, because of contamination of Iranian uranium with heavy metals, Iran cannot possibly enrich beyond even 20% without support from Russia or China [2]. IAEA director, Dr. Mohammad ElBaradei, too, has declared that there is no imminent threat and "We need to lower the pitch."

4. Iran has met its obligations under the Nuclear non-Proliferation Treaty (NPT). Iran has fully cooperated in the last three years with the IAEA and had voluntarily accepted and enforced safeguards well above the Additional Protocol until Iran's nuclear file was reported under the pressure of the US to the Security Council in February 2006. (The U.S., by contrast, has neither signed nor implemented the Additional Protocol, and Israel has refused to sign the NPT.)

Iran's earlier concealment of its nuclear programme took place in the context of the US-backed invasion of Iran by Saddam; Iraqi chemical weapons provided to Saddam by the US, German and UK companies with the approval of their governments which were used against Iranian soldiers and civilians and Israel's destruction of Iraq's Osirak reactor in 1981 with impunity. Iranian leaders concluded from these gross injustices that international laws are only "ink on paper" as Rafsanjani put it.

But the most direct reasons for Iran's concealment were the American trade embargo on Iran and Washington's organized and persistent campaign to stop civilian nuclear technology from reaching Iran from any source. For example, in 1995 Germany offered to let Kraftwerk Union (a subsidiary of Siemens) finish Iran's Bushehr reactor, but withdrew its proposal under US pressure [3]. The following year, China cancelled its contract to build a nuclear enrichment facility in Isfahan for the same reason [4]. Thus Washington systematically violated, with impunity, Article IV of the NPT, which allows signatories to "facilitate, and have the right to participate in, the fullest possible exchange of equipment, materials and scientific and technological information for the peaceful uses of nuclear energy".

Nevertheless, Iran's decision not to declare all of its nuclear installations did not violate any rules. According to David Albright and Corey Hinderstein, who first provided satellite imagery and analysis of the facilities at Natanz and at Arak in December 2002 [5], under the safeguards agreement in force at the time, "Iran is not required to allow IAEA inspections of a new nuclear facility until six months before nuclear material is introduced into it."

5. Iran has given unprecedented concessions on its nuclear programme. Unlike North Korea, Iran has resisted the temptation to withdraw from the NPT. Besides accepting snap inspections under Additional Protocol until February 2006, Iran has invited Western companies, including American companies, to participate in a consortium to develop Iran's civilian nuclear programme. Such joint ventures combined with Iran's pledge to ratify the Additional Protocol for

intrusive IAEA inspections, would create the best assurance that the enriched uranium would not be diverted to a weapons programme. Such concessions are very rare in the world, but the U.S. and its allies have refused Iran's offer.

6. Enrichment of uranium for a civilian nuclear programme is Iran's inalienable right. Every member of the NPT has the inalienable right to enrich uranium for a civilian nuclear programme and is entitled to full technical assistance.

But with the US as the back seat driver and in violation of their assistance obligations, France, Germany, and the UK insisted in three years of negotiations, that Tehran forfeit its right, in return for incentives of little value. Some European diplomats admitted to Asia Times-on-line on 7th September 2005, that the package offered by the EU-3 was "an empty box of chocolates." But "there is nothing else we can offer," the diplomats went on to say. "The Americans simply wouldn't let us."

7. The Western alliance has not tried true diplomacy. Washington has refused to participate in talks with Iran and instead outsourced the task to the EU. But negotiators for France, Britain, and Germany were hamstrung by the Bush Administration, which disapproved any substantive incentives, including a US guarantee not to attack Iran. This was the reason Iran ended its two-year voluntary suspension of uranium enrichment.

WESTERN HYPOCRISY

8. The UN resolutions against Iran in contrast to the treatment of South Korea, India, Pakistan, and Israel smack of double standards. The UN Security Council sanctions on Iran expose the double standards of the Western powers, which ignore the NPT violations by Washington's allies. For example, in the year 2000, South Korea enriched 200 milligrams of uranium to near-weapons grade (up to 77%), but was not referred to the UN Security Council.

India has refused to sign the NPT or allow inspections and has developed an atomic arsenal, but receives nuclear assistance from the US which is a violation of the NPT. More bizarrely, India has a seat on the governing board of IAEA and, under US pressure, voted to refer Iran as a violator to the UN Security Council. Another non-signatory, Pakistan, clandestinely developed nuclear weapons but is supported by the US as a "war on terror" ally.

Israel is a close ally of Washington, even though it has hundreds of clandestine nuclear weapons, has dismissed numerous UN resolutions and has refused to sign the NPT or open any of its nuclear plants to inspections.

The US itself is the most serious violator of the NPT. The only country to have ever used nuclear bombs in war has refused to reduce its nuclear arsenal, in violation of Article VI of NPT. The US is also in breach of the treaty because it is developing new generations of nuclear warheads for use against non-nuclear adversaries. Moreover, the US has deployed hundreds of such tactical nuclear weapons all around the world in violation of Articles I and II of the NPT.

9. Iran has not threatened Israel or attacked another country. The track records of the US, Israel, the UK and France are very different. These so called "democracies" have a bloody history of invading other countries for resources and domination. On the contrary, Iran's supreme leader, Ayatollah Khamenei, has stated repeatedly that Iran will not attack or threaten any country. He has also issued a fatwa against the production, stockpiling and use of nuclear weapons and banned nuclear weapons as sacrilegious. Iran has been a consistent supporter of the Nuclear non-Proliferation Treaty (NPT) and called for a nuclear weapons free Middle East.

The comments of Iran's President Ahmadinejad against Israel have been repeated statesmen since 1979 and indicate no practical threat. The statement attributed to him that "Israel should be wiped off the map" has been reported by Jonathan Steele in the Guardian and by Professor Juan Cole, amongst other Farsi language experts, to have been a mistranslation and these clarifications have been widely disseminated. What he actually said was "the regime occupying Jerusalem must vanish from the page of time". Ahmadinejad has made clear that he envisions regime change in Israel through internal decay, similar to fashion of the demise of the Soviet Union. Iranian leaders have said consistently for two decades that they will accept a two-state solution in Palestine if a majority of Palestinians favour that option.

This is in sharp contrast to the explicit threats by Israeli and the US leaders against Iran, including current operations to destabilize the Islamic Republic as described by Seymour Hersh [6] and plans to foment ethnic unrest and separatist movements to wipe Iran off the map [7].

Iran is no match for Israel, whose security and military needs are all but guaranteed by the US. Iran is surrounded on all sides by the US Navy and American bases. The Western media try to portray a picture which is quite opposite to the truth. The threat to security and stability in the region comes not from Iran but from the US, whose forces have occupied Afghanistan and Iraq and from Israel which continues its illegal occupation of Palestinian land.

Iran has not invaded or threatened any country for two and a half centuries. The only war the Islamic Republic fought was the one imposed by Saddam's army, which invaded Iran with the backing of the US and its allies. When Iraq used chemical weapons, supplied by the West, against Iranian soldiers, Iran did not retaliate in kind. When the Taliban regime murdered eight Iranian diplomats in 1996 and remained unapologetic, Iran did not respond militarily.

10. The US "democratization" programme for Iran is a hoax. Although violations of human rights and democratic freedoms do occur too often in Iran, the country has the most pluralistic system in a region dominated by undemocratic client states of the US. It is sheer hypocrisy for the US, which turns a blind eye to the gross human rights abuses by its client states, such as Turkmenistan,

Pakistan, Saudi Arabia, Israel, Libya, and Egypt, to misrepresent its agenda in Iran as a "democratization" programme. Washington's pretensions ring especially hollow when one remembers that in 1953 Iran's nascent democracy under Prime Minister Mohammad Mossadeq was overthrown by the CIA, which restored a hated military dictatorship for the benefit of American oil conglomerates.

UN SECURITY COUNCIL INVOLVEMENT TOTALLY UNJUSTIFIED

11. There are no legal bases for Iran's referral to the UN Security Council. Since there is no evidence that Iran is even contemplating its nuclear programme, no grounds exist within the NPT to refer Iran to the UN Security Council.

Michael Spies of the New York-based Lawyers' Committee on Nuclear Policy has clarified the issue: "Under the Statute (Art. 12(C)) and the Safeguards Agreement, the Board may only refer Iran to the Security Council if it finds that, based on the report from the Director General, it cannot be assured that Iran has not diverted nuclear material for non-peaceful purpose. In the past, findings of `non-assurance' have only come in the face of a history of active and ongoing non-cooperation with IAEA safeguards. The pursuit of nuclear activities in itself, which is specifically recognized as a sovereign right, and which remain safeguarded, could not legally or logically equate to uncertainty regarding diversion." [8]

Dr ElBradei has consistently confirmed that there has been no diversion of safeguarded nuclear material in Iran. He has also said, under pressure from Washington, that he cannot rule out the existence of undeclared nuclear activities in the country. However, according to the IAEA's Safeguards Implementation Report for 2005 (issued on 15 June 2006), 45 other countries, including 14 European countries, in particular Germany, are in this same category as Iran. Moreover, according to the UK-based Campaign for Nuclear Disarmament, such findings and a clear bill for any given country will take an average of six years of inspections and verification by the IAEA. In the case of Iran, these investigations have been going on for only about four years now.

Thus, all concerns regarding Iran's nuclear programme must be dealt with under the auspices of the IAEA. The US and its allies violated the rules by exerting massive pressure on the IAEA to report Iran without any legitimacy to the UN Security Council. In fact, David Mulford, the US Ambassador to India, warned the Government of India in January 2006 that there would be no US-India nuclear deal if India did not vote against Iran in the Governors' Board of the IAEA. On February 15th 2007, Stephen Rademaker, the former US Assistant Secretary for International Security and Non-proliferation, confessed that the US coerced India to vote against Iran in the two crucial meetings of the IAEA in 2005 and 2006 which resulted in Iran's file to be reported to the UN Security Council. This shows clearly that reporting Iran to the UN Security Council and the subsequent adoption of the Security Council Resolutions 1696 and 1737 have been carried out with US coercion and have thus no legitimacy at all [9].

SANCTIONS NOT A GOOD IDEA

12. Dr ElBradei, the head of the IAEA, has said that sanctions are counterproductive. Economic sanctions on Iran will harm the people of Iran, as they were devastating to Iraqis, resulting in the death of at least 500,000 children. Sanctions would not however bring the Islamic Republic to its knees. Instead, any kind of sanctions, including the so-called targeted or smart sanctions, are viewed by the Iranian people as the West's punishment for Iran's scientific progress (uranium enrichment for reactor fuel). As sanctions tighten, nationalist fervour will strengthen the resolve of Iranians to defend the country's civilian nuclear programme.

13. Sanctions are not better than war; they are a prelude to bombing. Sanctions are increasing tensions in the region and can soon push the dispute to the point of no return. Since sanctions do not exert significant pressure on the Iranian government, they only pave the

way for the illegal use of force against Iran, as they did in Iraq. Thus, countries which support sanctions against Iran are only falling into the US trap in aiding the war drive on Iran.

ILLEGALITY OF A MILITARY ATTACK

14. Foreign state interference in Iran violates the UN charter. The US is reported, for example by Seymour Hersh in the 17th April 2006 issue of the New Yorker, to be running covert operations in Iran to foment unrest and ethnic conflict for the purpose of regime change. Unmanned US drones have also entered into Iranian air space to spy over Iranian military installations and to map Iranian radar systems. These actions violate the UN Charter's guarantee of the right of self-determination for all nations.

The Bush Administration has also confirmed, in the 2006 US National Security Strategy, its long term policy for pre-emptive military action against its adversaries. Tony Blair supported this policy in his 21st March 2006 foreign policy speech. However, unprovoked strikes are illegal under international law. To remove this obstacle, John Reid, the British Secretary of Defence, in his speech on 3rd April 2006 to the Royal United Services Institute for Defense and Security Studies, proposed a change in international law on pre-emptive military action.

Reports of nuclear attack scenarios by the US or Israel against Iran can serve to raise the public's tolerance for an act of aggression with conventional military means. People of conscience must therefore not only condemn a possible nuclear attack as the maddest of criminal insanities by the Bush Administration, but also denounce any conventional assault.

UNINTENDED CONSEQUENCES OF AN ATTACK ON IRAN

15. A military attack on Iran could sharply raise the price of oil. A US or Israeli attack on Iran would, according to Iranian government

leaders, provoke immediate retaliation by Tehran, which may include a blockade of the Persian Gulf. Such a response could cause a major disruption in energy markets and double the price of oil, with a global economic depression to follow.

16. Bombing cannot end Iran's nuclear programme. Since Iran already has the expertise to enrich uranium up to the 3.5% grade for a fuel cycle, no degree of bombing will halt Iran's civilian nuclear programme. On the contrary, the resulting mass casualties and destruction would strengthen the voices that argue Iran, like North Korea, should build a nuclear deterrent.

17. A nuclear attack on Iran would fuel a new nuclear arms race and ruin the NPT. Washington has in recent years blurred the distinction between conventional and nuclear weapons in its military strategy declarations, including in the Doctrine for Joint Nuclear Operations, which now allow the US to employ its nuclear arsenal against non-nuclear countries if they are not in compliance with the NPT.

Many leaked policy discussions indicate that the US will consider it "justified" to repeat its act of genocide in Hiroshima and Nagasaki and use tactical nuclear bombs to destroy hardened Iranian targets. Ominously, President Bush has characterized these as "wild speculation" but has not denied them.

18. An attack on Iran will unite Iranians against the US and its allies. A great majority of the public in Iran support the country's right to enrich uranium for civilian purposes. Therefore, a bombing campaign will not lead to an uprising by the Iranian people for regime change as envisaged by the US. Rather, it would ignite nationalist feelings in the country and unite the population, including most of the government's critics, against the West.

19. An attack on Iran will lead to a regional catastrophe and expanded terrorism. Senator McCain, the Republican presidential hopeful, who has himself advocated the use of force on Iran, has predicted that an attack against Iran will lead to Armageddon. Hosni Mubarak, the

President of Egypt, has also strongly warned the US against an attack. American or Israeli aggression on Iran, coming on the heels of the Iraq disaster, would inflame the passions of Muslims worldwide and help jihadi extremists with their recruitment campaign. The region wide conflagration that an Israel/US attack on Iran would create will dwarf the catastrophe that US-UK led invasion of Iraq has brought up for the people of Iraq [10].

20. The cause of establishing democracy in Iran will suffer gravely if the country is attacked. President Bush's "axis of evil" rhetoric severely undermined the reformist movement in Iran at a time when the country's president promoted Dialogue Among Civilizations. Bush's hostile posture strengthened the hands of Iranian hardliners and led to the reformist movement's electoral defeat. That setback would be dwarfed by the consequences of a military assault on the country. Iran's burgeoning civil society would be among the first victims of US or Israeli aggression.

This is precisely why leading reformists and human rights activists in Iran, such as the popular Nobel Laureate, Shirin Ebadi, have strongly opposed sanctions and military interventions against Iran. By contrast, the Mojahedin-e Khalgh (MEK), which has no support in the country and is listed as a terrorist organization by the EU and the US, can have a future only if all democratic rights are totally suppressed in Iran. The CIA and the Pentagon support MEK in covert operations to destabilize the Islamic Republic [11].

References:

[1] http://www.payvand.com/news/03/oct/1015.html
[2] http://www.oxfordresearchgroup.org.uk/publications/briefings/IranNuclear.htm
[3] http://www.payvand.com/news/03/oct/1039.html
[4] http://en.wikipedia.org/wiki/Iran's_nuclear_program
[5] http://www.isis-online.org/publications/iran/iranimages.html
[6] http://www.newyorker.com/fact/content/articles/060417fa_fact

[7]   http://news.ft.com/cms/s/ed436938-a49d-11da-897c-0000779e2340,s01=1.html

[8] http://svaradarajan.blogspot.com/2006/03/sawers-letter-game-plan-on-iran-is.html

[9] http://www.campaigniran.org/casmii/index.php?q=node/1545

[10] http://news.bbc.co.uk/1/hi/world/middle_east/6464277.stm

[11] http://www.campaigniran.org/casmii/index.php?q=node/1645

Is the Israel Lobby Pushing the United States?

The issues they [Mearsheimer and Walt] raise are all the more relevant these days because of the crescendo of calls for American and/or Israeli military attacks to halt Iran's nuclear industry development. They see troubling parallels between the lobby's push for the US attack against Iraq -- "one of the greatest strategic blunders in American history," Mearsheimer calls it -- and the current drive by Israel and the pro-Israel lobby to nudge Washington to do something similar against Iran.

Things to Consider before Attacking Iran

Possible American moves against Iran should be considered in light of the 2001-2007 lessons of US-led wars to change regimes and remake national governance systems in Afghanistan and Iraq -- and indirectly in Palestine and Lebanon. This is not just a Bush-Cheney problem: This is an all-American problem, since most presidential candidates in both parties do not stray far from the administration's aggressive policy options.

Subject: LETTER TO THE EDITOR, FROM A DEMOCRAT

MONEY, DONATIONS, AMERICA'S MANDATE.

Money is a very important commodity, we have given and given in support of the Democrat party.

We gave enough to regain control of congress 2006 elections, that came with a well know mandate. A mandate to end the WAR, end the corruption in government. To reform the campaigns, and to prosecute the WAR crimes.

Now you continue to ask for more money, while you do not do the job, paid for in advance.

Now corporate money, foreign lobbies and organized crime influences you all more, thus our mandate goes unfulfilled.

PLEASE, don't ask for more, until the job we paid for and voted for is done.

YES, we the people still give, we may not have the influence of special interest you all bow down to.

BUT, we give to the candidates that do not take money from the corrupt, and consider us the American people their special interest. That will end this war, that will bring our troops home, that will prosecute the corrupt. That will protect our borders, that will respond to Americans needs.

That being, a campaign of OBAMA & EDWARDS. If we don't get that ticket, we do not give, we do not vote. WE trust no one else to take OUR country BACK. Honor, Integrity, True moral values, an agenda for America not AIPAC, that will bring respect back internationally.

That will make every attempt to fulfill the MANDATE of the AMERICAN people.

Any thing, or Any one else is just more of the same.

Ronald L. Waldron
48 Hammond Street
Jamestown, NY 14701

716-483-5583
rwaldron@stny.rr.com

www.ingramcontent.com/pod-product-compliance
Lightning Source LLC
Chambersburg PA
CBHW061356280526
45784CB00001B/276